THE OLD
KINGSTON ROAD

K. KIRKHAM,

THE OLD KINGSTON ROAD

PHOTOGRAPHS BY
PAUL VON BAICH

INTRODUCTION BY
JENNIFER Mc KENDRY

Toronto
OXFORD UNIVERSITY PRESS
1980

Designed by FORTUNATO AGLIALORO

© Oxford University Press (Canadian Branch) 1980
ISBN 0-19-540304-5

1 2 3 4 — 3 2 1 0

Printed in Hong Kong by
EVERBEST PRINTING COMPANY LIMITED

INTRODUCTION
by Jennifer McKendry

Through the images presented here by Paul von Baich we are able to heighten our awareness of the past in the present and can better visualize our place in the changing pattern of history. The region of the Old Kingston Road, which follows the north shore of the St Lawrence River from the Quebec border and along Lake Ontario to Toronto, has a history of European colonization that goes back into the seventeenth century. The Sun King, Louis XIV, ruled the French Empire when Fort Frontenac, now Kingston, was established in 1673 at the strategic junction of the Great Cataraqui River; the St Lawrence, and Lake Ontario.

With the end of the French régime in 1763, the taming of the forests of Ontario was hastened by the arrival in 1784 of the first United Empire Loyalists, seeking refuge from the American Revolution. The bush fell prey to the white man's fear of deep-shaded regions. Where immense trees once kept the sun from the forest floor, crops soon triumphed.

The thin line of Loyalist farms and towns, clinging to the river bank and lake, wavered under American attack during the War of 1812. Pockets of settlement, such as Gananoque and Brockville, were raided by the enemy, and many fine Georgian-styled houses destroyed. However, as happens in war, some people thrived, particularly in Kingston, where tremendous ship-building activities boosted the town's economy.

Not until 1836, when Fort Henry was rebuilt in stone, were Kingston's defenses properly tightened. The fort was essential at that time to protect the outlet of the new Rideau Canal –an impressive engineering feat that was built from Ottawa to Kingston, so that troops passing through could bypass the St Lawrence River, which was vulnerable to American aggression. The canal also opened up the back country to new settlers who poured forth from Great Britain after the 1812 war. Motives for emigration varied: one of the most tragic migrations was that of the Irish who fled the 1847 potato famine in their homeland, only to fall victim in Canada to cholera, which also killed many residents who came in contact with the newcomers.

After the Rebellion of 1837, the population grew, towns expanded, and new farmlands were opened up. Parts of the rural areas, villages, and towns along the Kingston Road still reflect this era. Domestic, religious, and civic buildings have survived well, but early industrial structures, which were unable to withstand technological advancement, are crumbling. It is moving to see decaying grist, lumber or textile mills around which the economy of an area once pivoted.

Entrepreneurs of the 1830s and 1840s turned raw goods such as wheat, flax, and wool into finished products and controlled their merchandising by operating local retail stores. While their 'empires' may have fallen, a few splendid houses built from their profits still stand. In some of them finely curved staircases link lower reception halls to formal upstairs ballrooms, as in the 1831 brick mansion of John and Henrietta McDonald in Gananoque, which now serves as the town hall. In other handsome buildings Neo-Classical mouldings are to be seen, for example, in the Alphaeus Jones House in Prescott, the Barnum House in Grafton, and the Macaulay House in Picton. But some impressive buildings, such as the 1831 Counter House in Kingston, have been demolished. It remains to be seen whether the irony of replacing these beautiful nineteenth-century buildings with parking lots and high-rises will sadden our descendants as deeply as it saddens us.

Bishop Mountain, an early visitor to Kingston, described in 1794 town buildings clustered near the waterfront and 'the hanging woods upon the hills behind'. In a sense this description still holds. Of course the perimeters of the city have grown and pushed the bush further and further back, but an easy drive takes you to areas where wolf howls evoke the sound of the wild. And when you follow the shores of the St Lawrence River and vast Lake Ontario, its waves drumming and spitting on the shore, as they have done for aeons, eroding rocks and pebbles to a sensuous smoothness, your mind drifts to imagine how this region must have seemed to the nomadic Mississauga and Iroquois; the French explorers, missionaries, and voyageurs; the Loyalist and European immigrants. It must have been both fearsome and beautiful.

By the time Kingston was declared the capital of the United Canadas in 1841, the colony was becoming increasingly sophisticated, as attested to by the remarks on the new capital's 'provincialism' by the legislators who were summoned to it. Inadequate housing had been a common complaint of the visitors, who came by stagecoach or steamboat. Now, as Kingston peaked in its golden age, new stone buildings were being erected at an astonishing rate. The City Hall, one of the largest buildings in British North America, was being built on the market square, its proud classical façade and dome facing Lake Ontario, and the rear wing, called the Market Shambles, pushing into the city's commercial section. But by the time it was completed in 1844, the capital had been moved to Montreal and the city's moment of glory was over. The building boom left many local investors teetering on the brink of financial disaster; fortunately there were steadying factors in the economy, such as trans-shipping, ship-building and repair; and the military presence. However, technological changes in the province's transportation system, among them new canals and railway lines, spelt doom for the city's conservative shipping *business. The withdrawal of the Imperial garrison in 1870 marked the end of an era.*

One result of these impediments to development and prosperity in Kingston is that the city has been preserved for us, unlike Toronto and Ottawa, where development has brought about the destruction of many heritage buildings. Even Fort Henry, which was virtually abandoned in the late nineteenth century, was restored in the 1930s and is today much visited by tourists.

The Fort is an obvious heritage project. More susceptible to change is the profile of old cities and towns. Until the beginning of the 1980s, the 1843 Kingston City Hall dominated the skyline and set the tone of the city, giving it an air of self-confidence. However, high-rise development on the waterfront will soon alter this profile. Having lost the battle for overall preservation, we are forced to concentrate on pockets of heritage buildings, which fortunately are numerous. Thus in one block (King, Clarence, Wellington, and Johnson Streets), we can find four limestone buildings that are significant in Ontario's architectural history: the Customs House, the Old Post Office, St George's Cathedral, and Church Hall.

Kingston shares with other early towns – including Brockville, Cobourg, and Prescott – suggestions of the past that can only be glimpsed when wandering through streets designed for horses and wagons: stables, hitching posts, well troughs, or spur stones canted to protect house corners from wagon wheels; walled gardens that can be seen through the shadowed stone arches of carriageways; cast- and wrought-iron footscrapers, from the days when streets were often mired in mud in wet weather; massive fireplace chimneys blocked against the sky or slender, fanciful chimneys for woodstove use.

We are the descendants of grandparents whose own grandparents pioneered along the Kingston Road. They imposed their European ways on the land but soon modified them into a Canadian tradition. Most were of British and German stock; firm beliefs and peasant strength helped them to survive the harsh conditions of the old world and sustained them in the rigours of the new where, at least, they could possess that ultimate treasure – land. The way in which they transformed the bushland and waterways of southeastern Ontario into thriving rural and urban settlements has coloured our vision of ourselves and made us cherish all reminders of that achievement.

THE OLD KINGSTON ROAD celebrates a part of Canada where a great many links with our past still exist. Seen through the discerning eye of an artist such as Paul von Baich, they make up a heritage of beauty and delight.

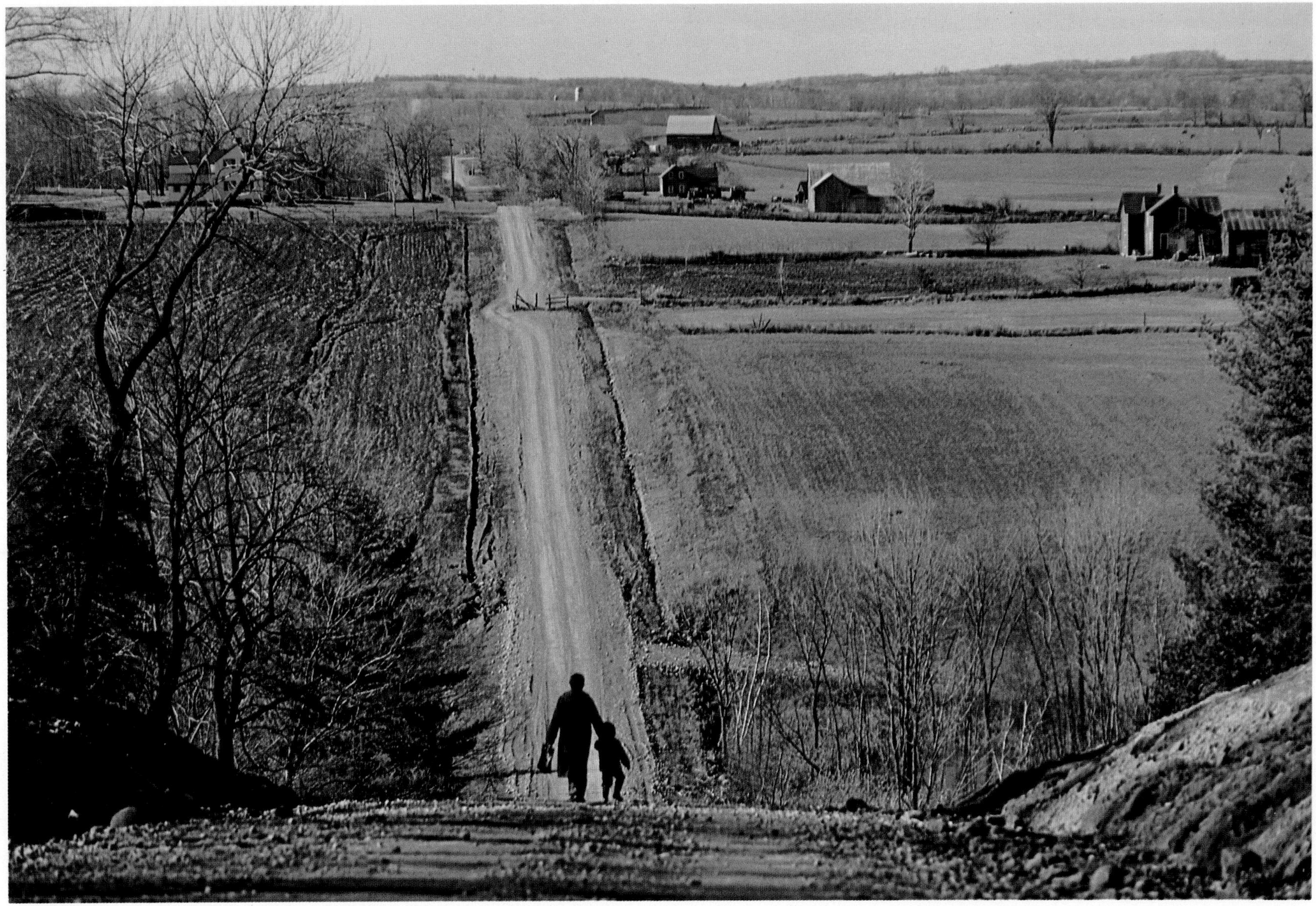

1 Off Godolphin Road

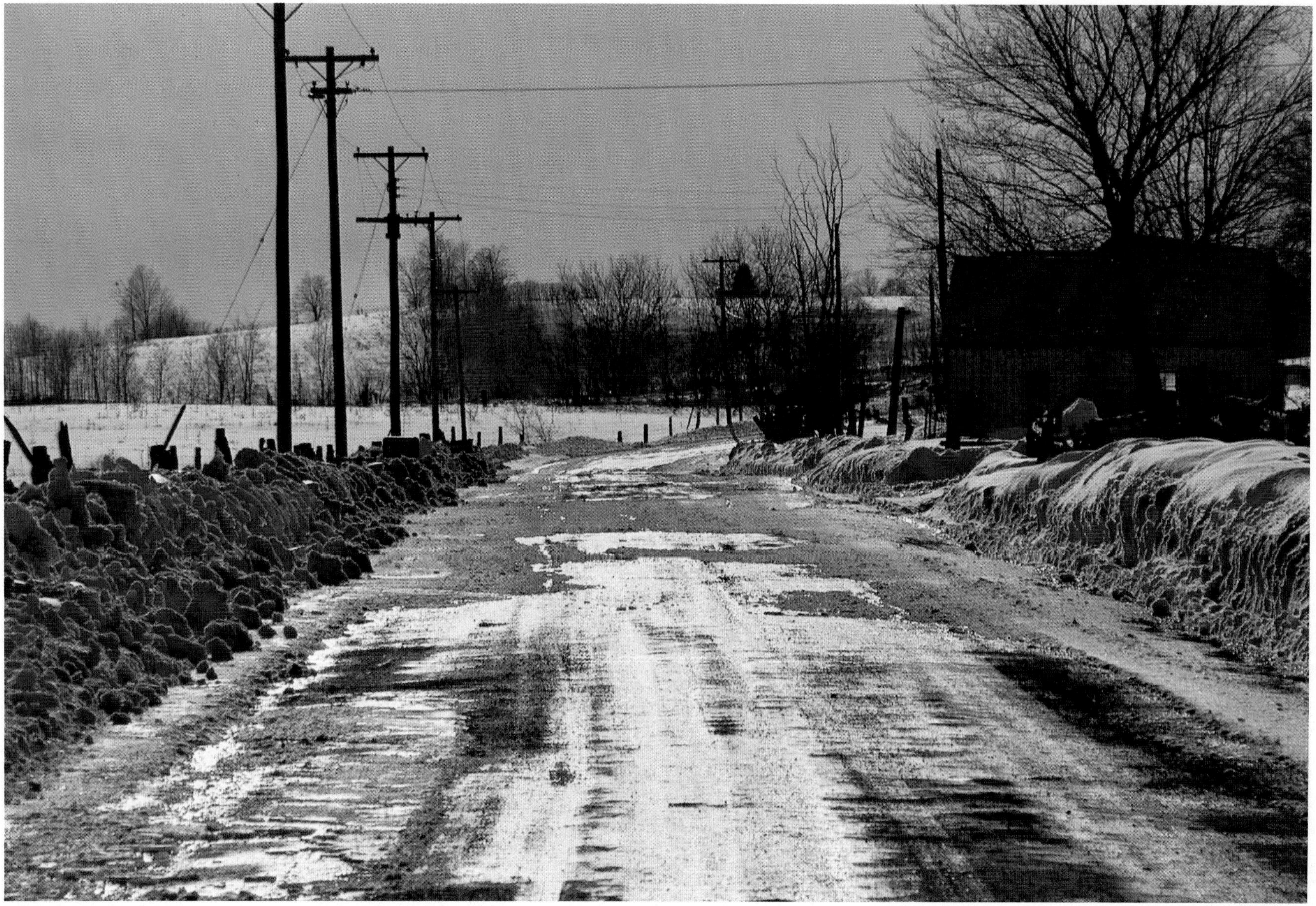

2 R.R. 1, Warkworth
3 Outlet Beach Provincial Park

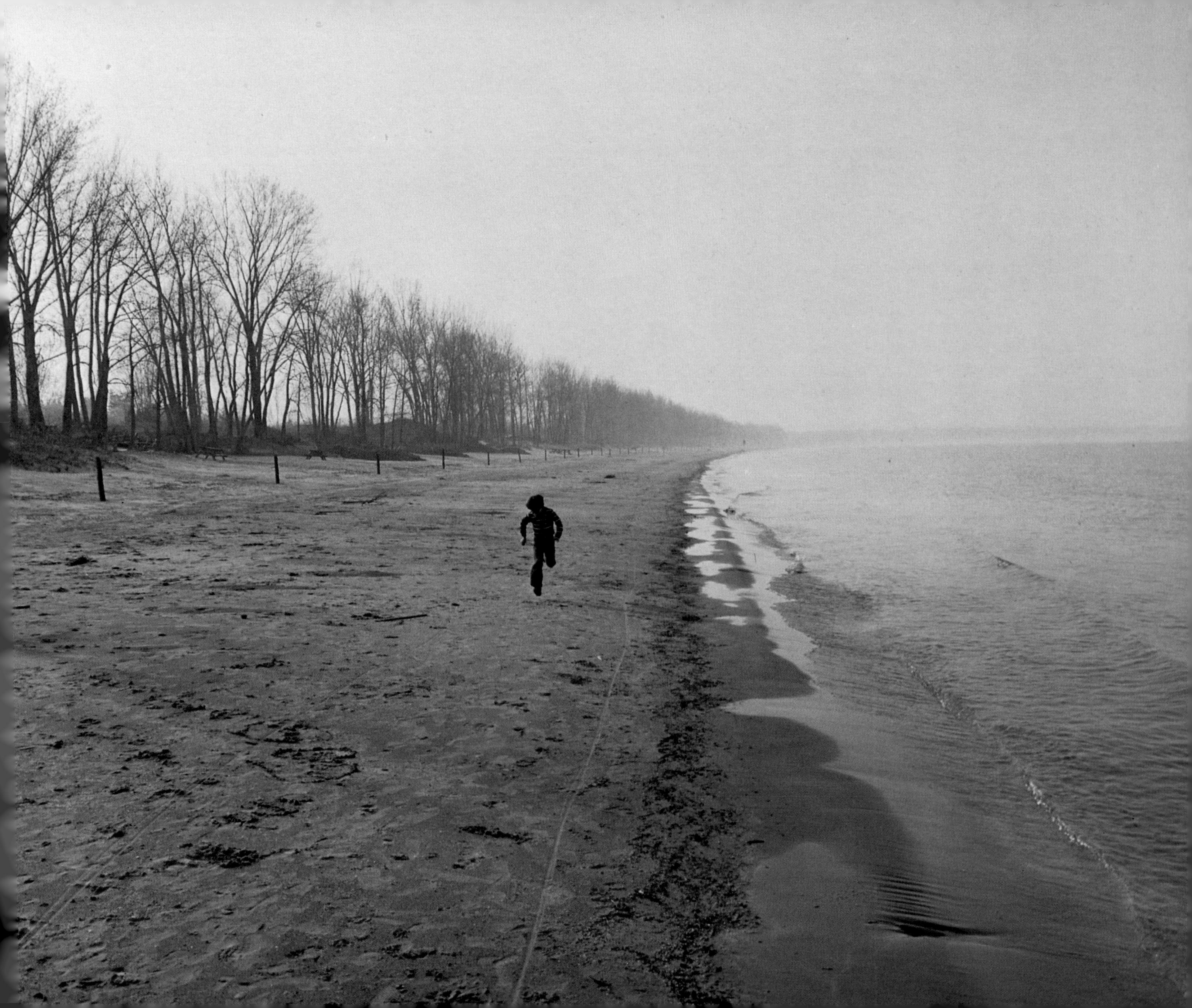

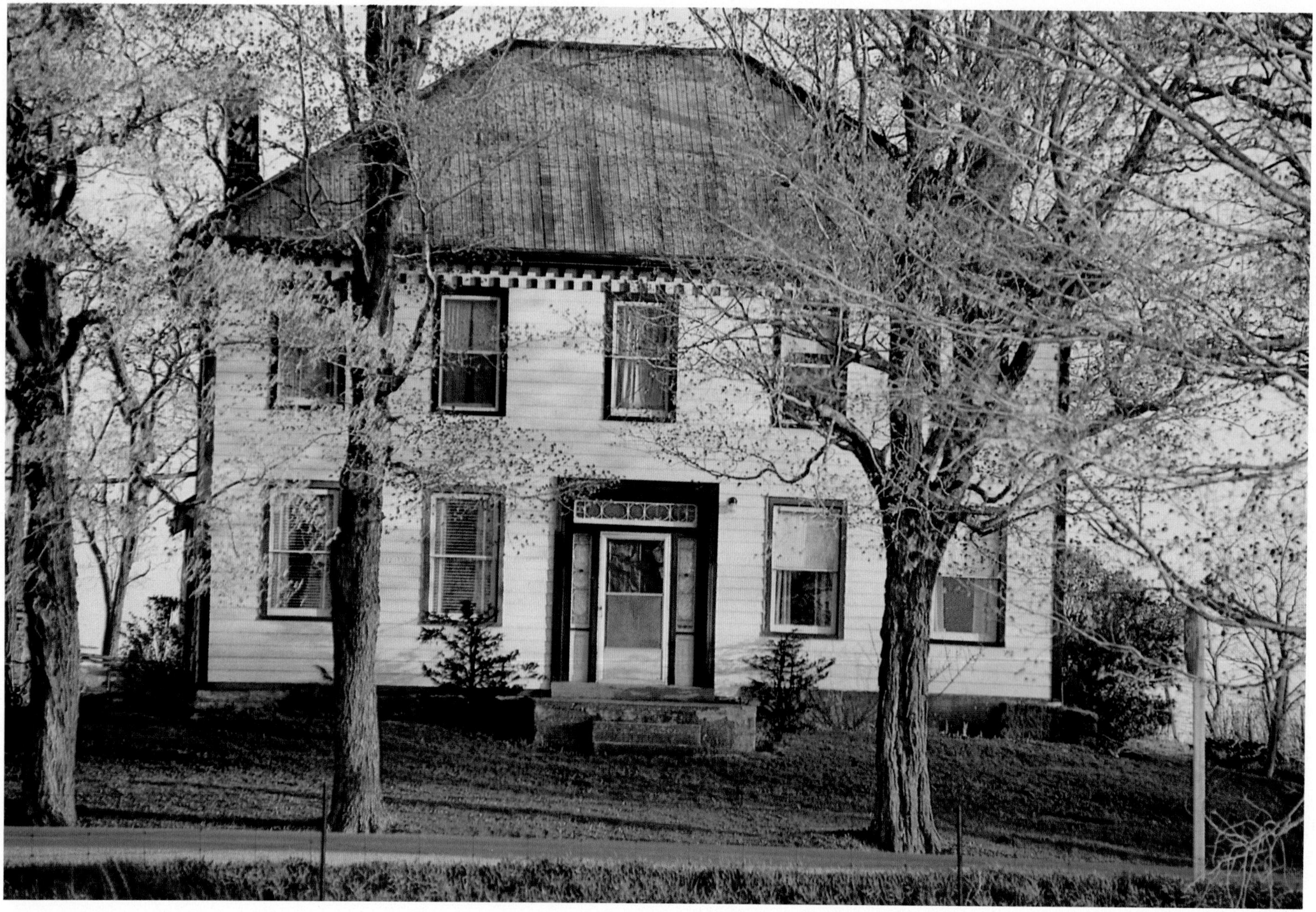

4 Near Mountain View
5 Near Rossmore

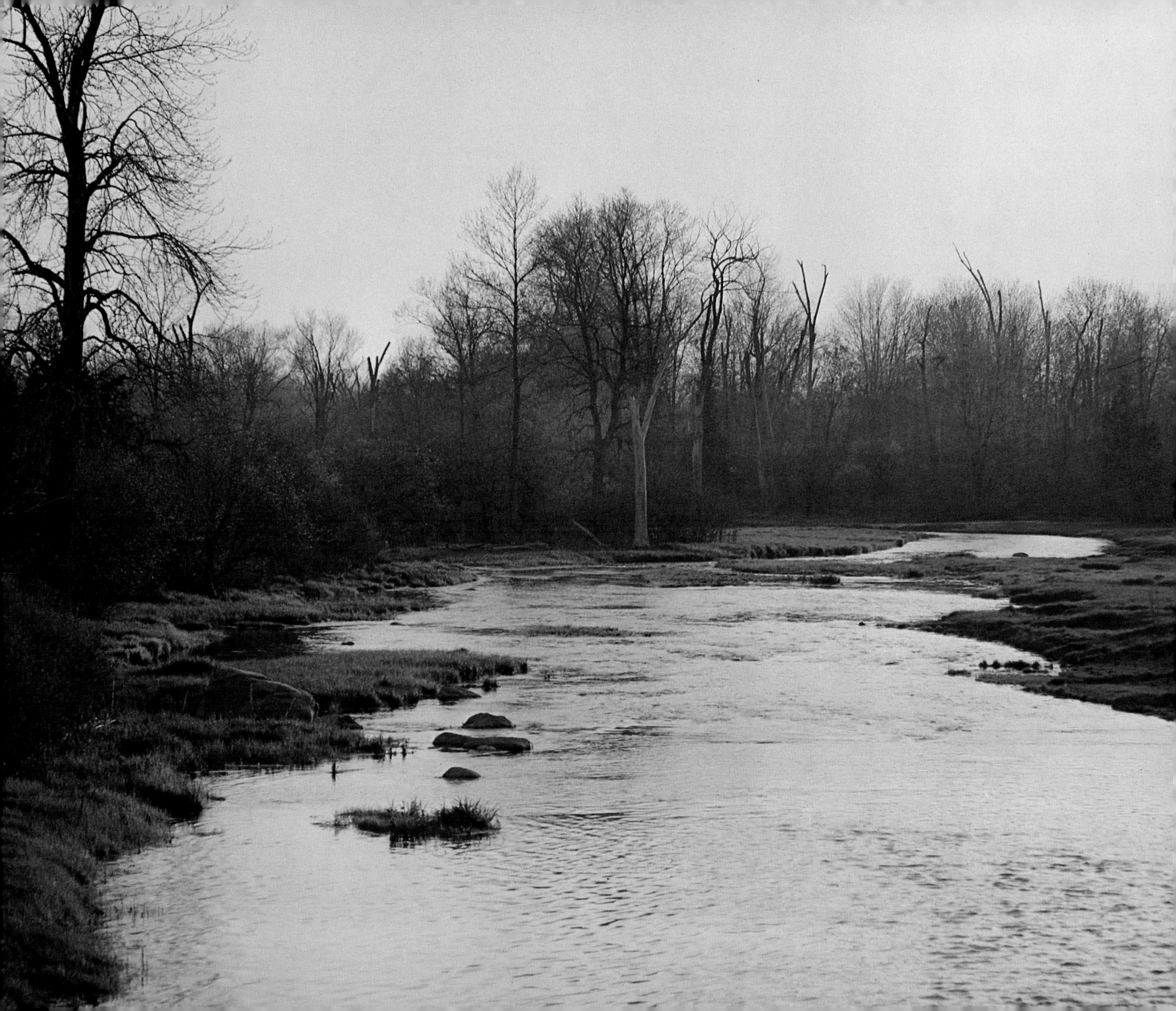

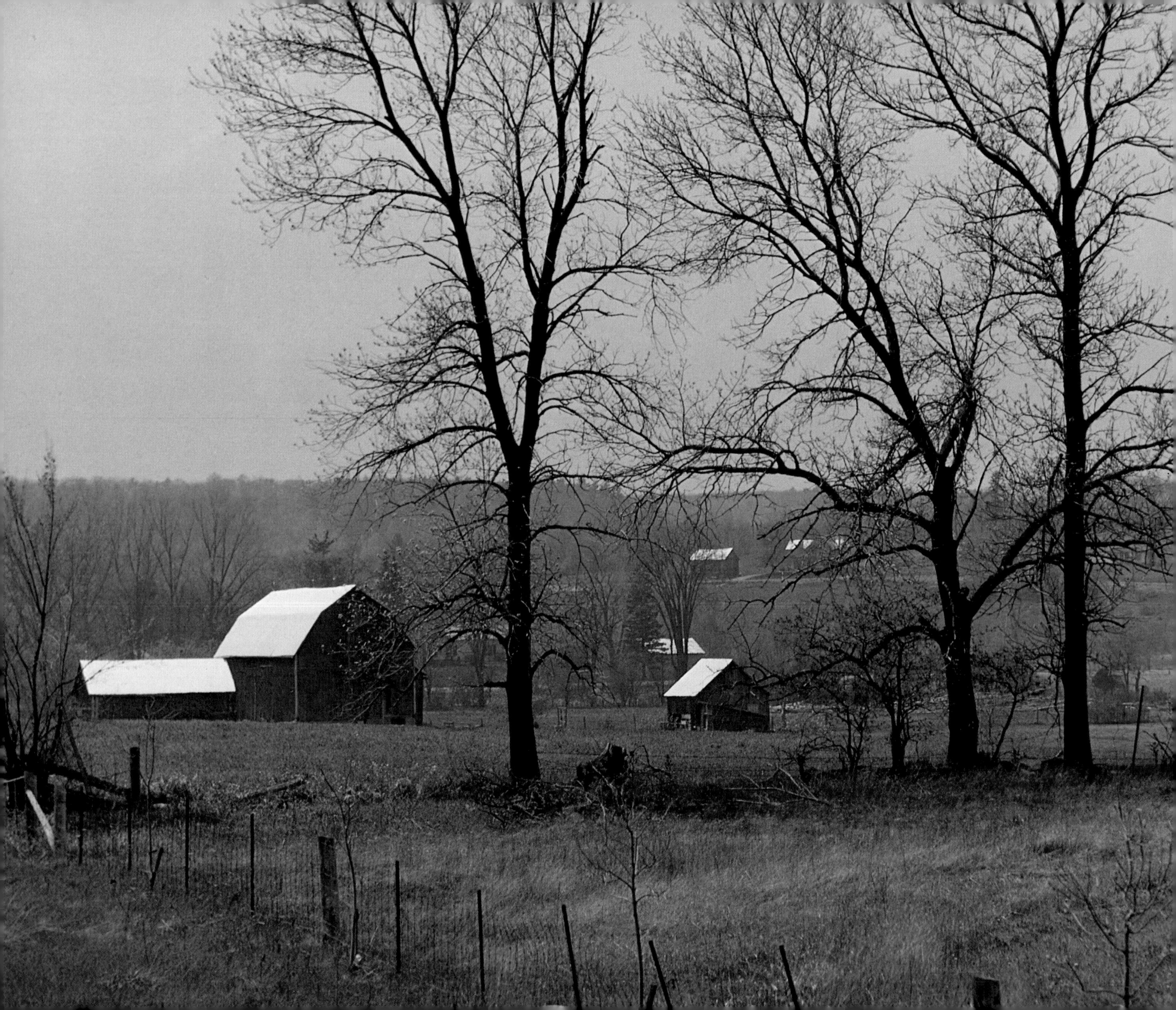

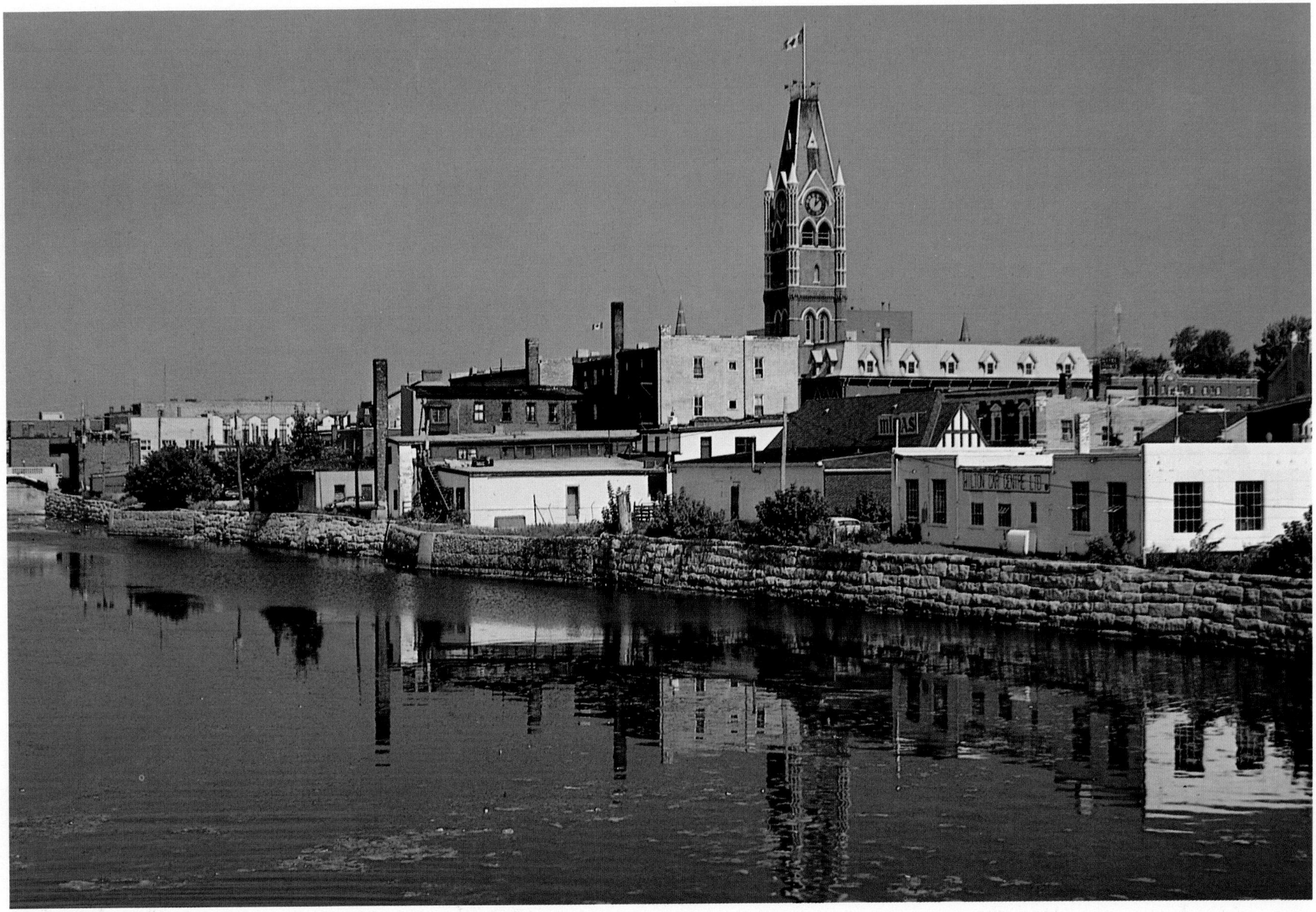

6 Near Stirling
7 Belleville

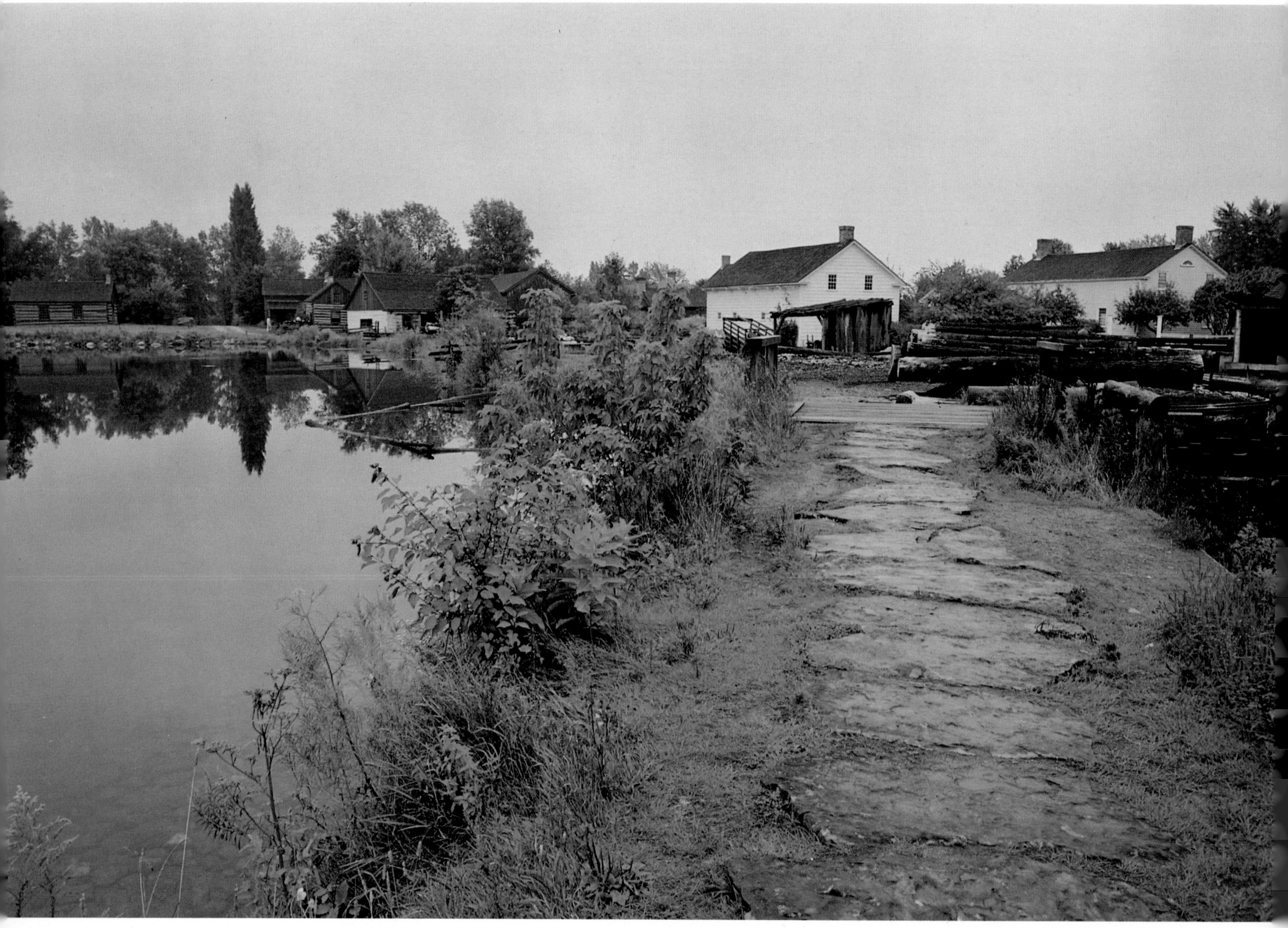

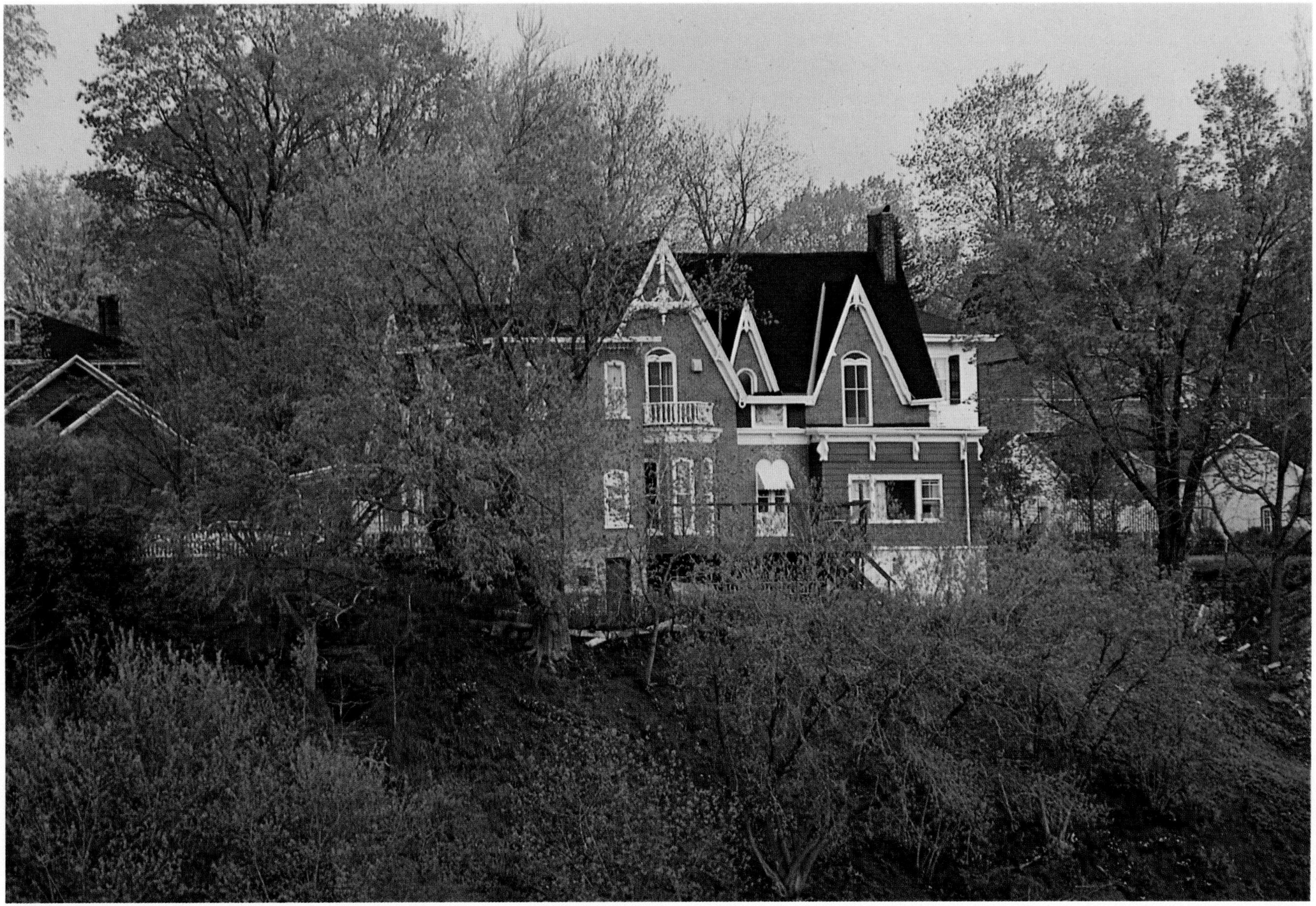

8 Upper Canada Village, Morrisburg
9 Picton

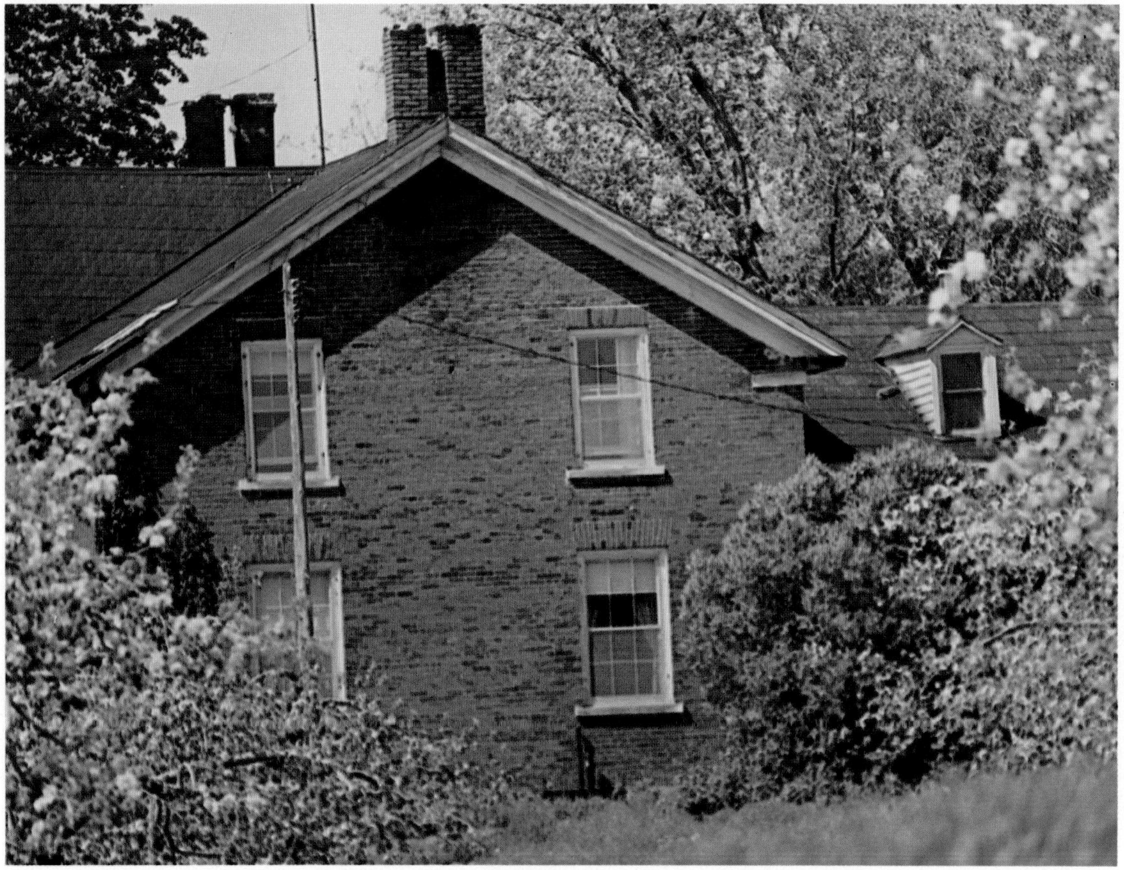

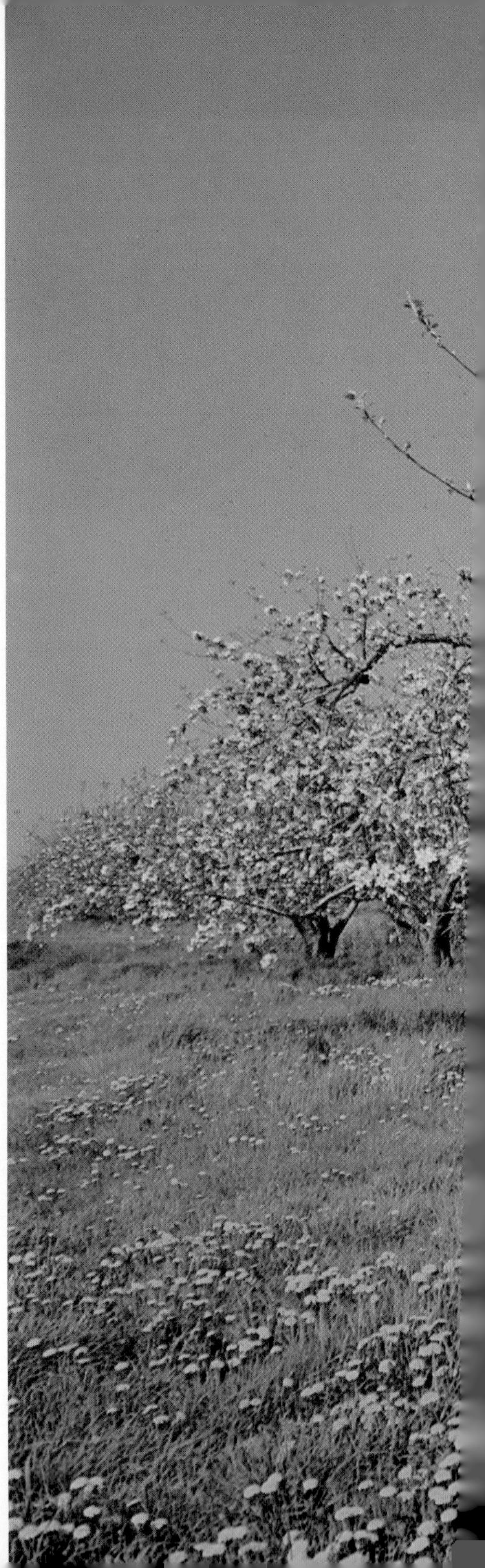

10 & 11 Brighton

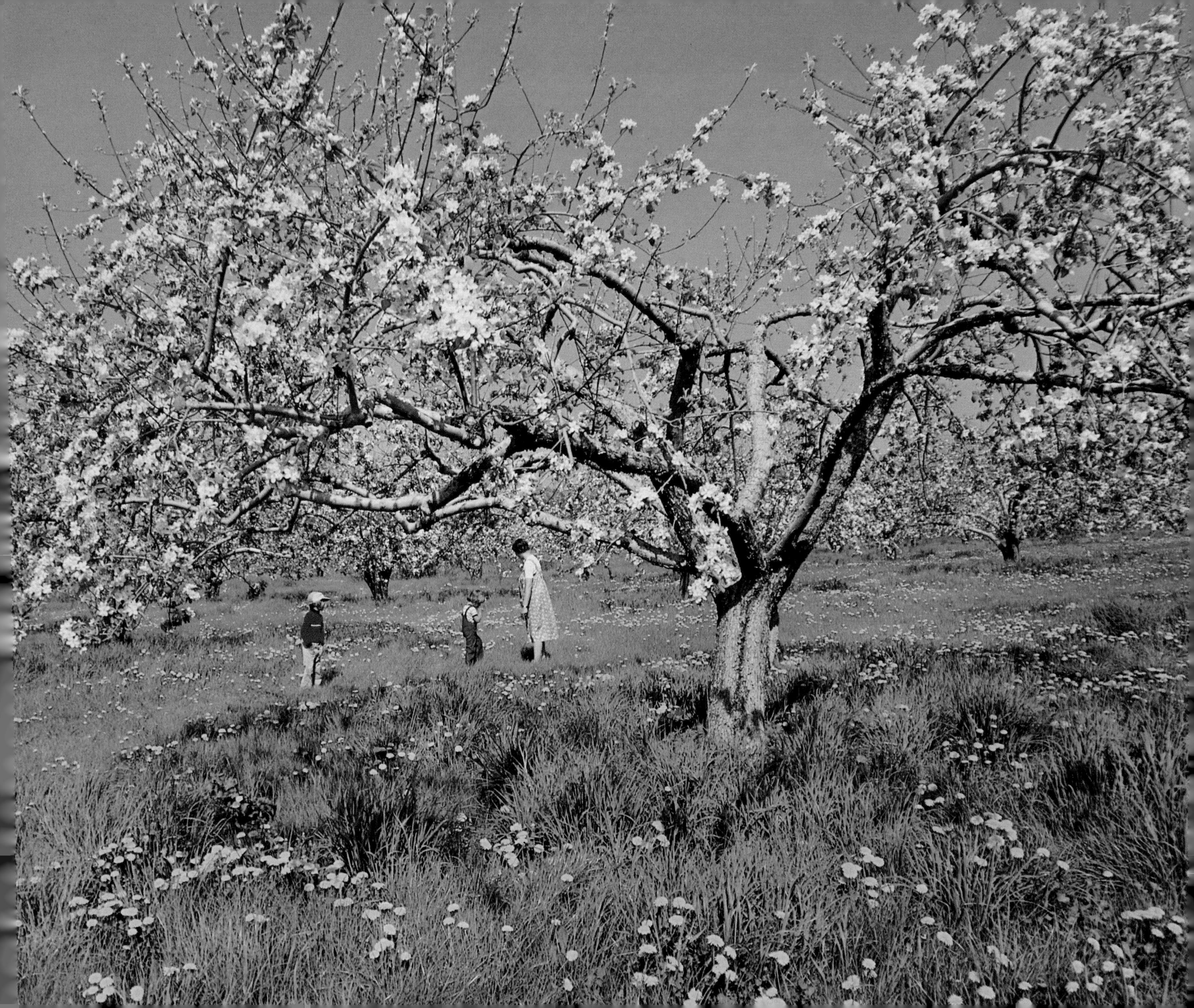

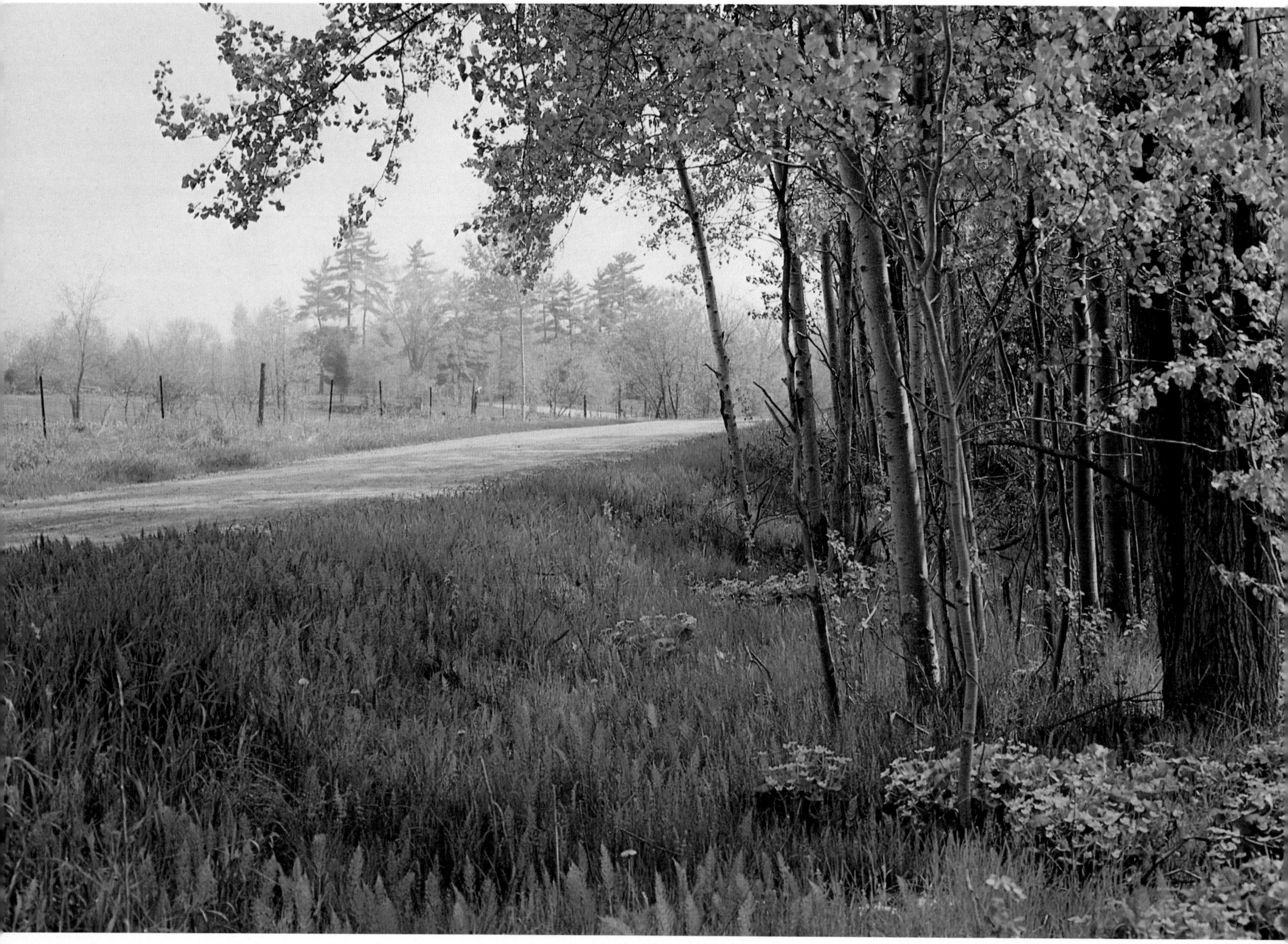

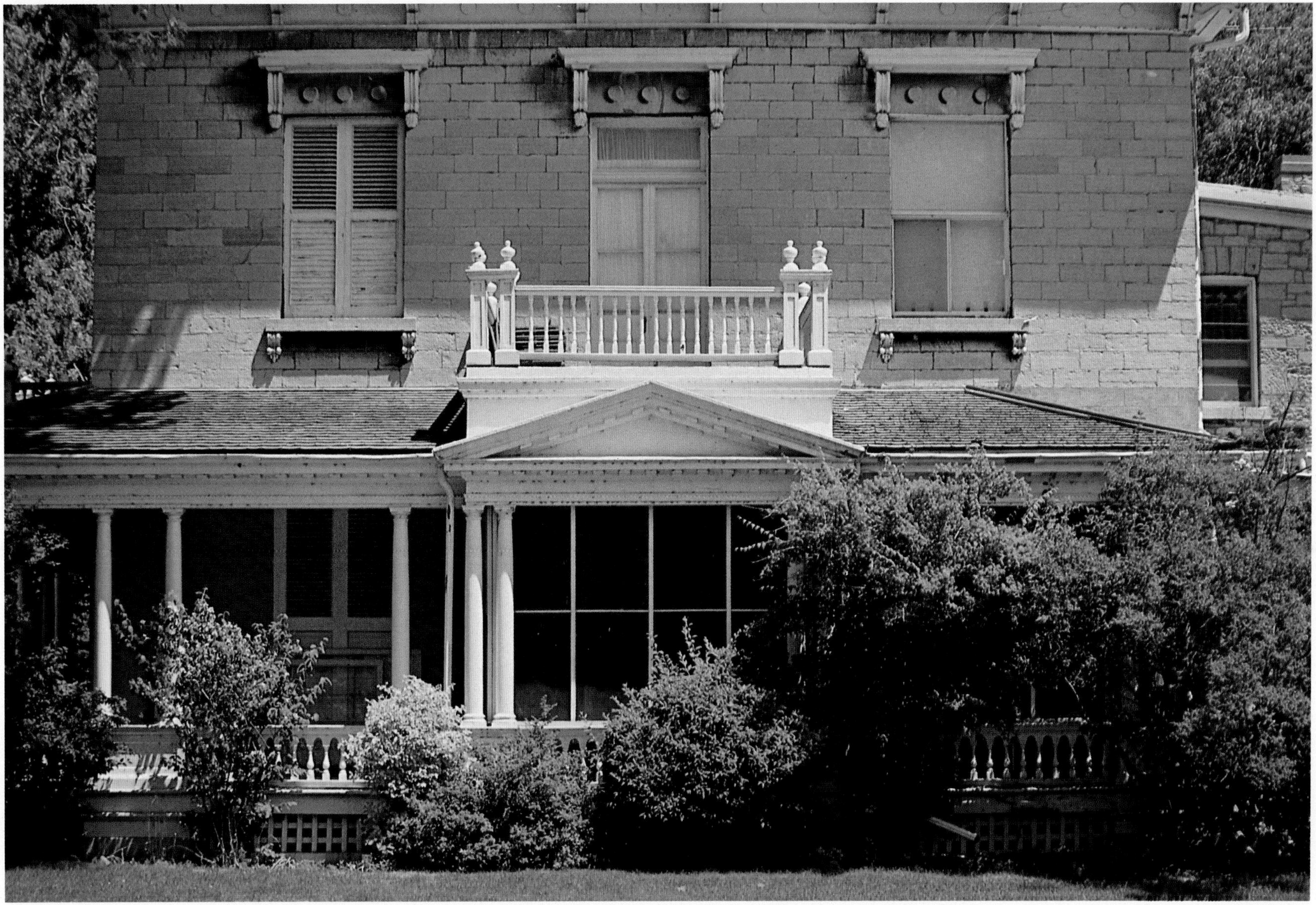

12 Percy Township
13 Kingston

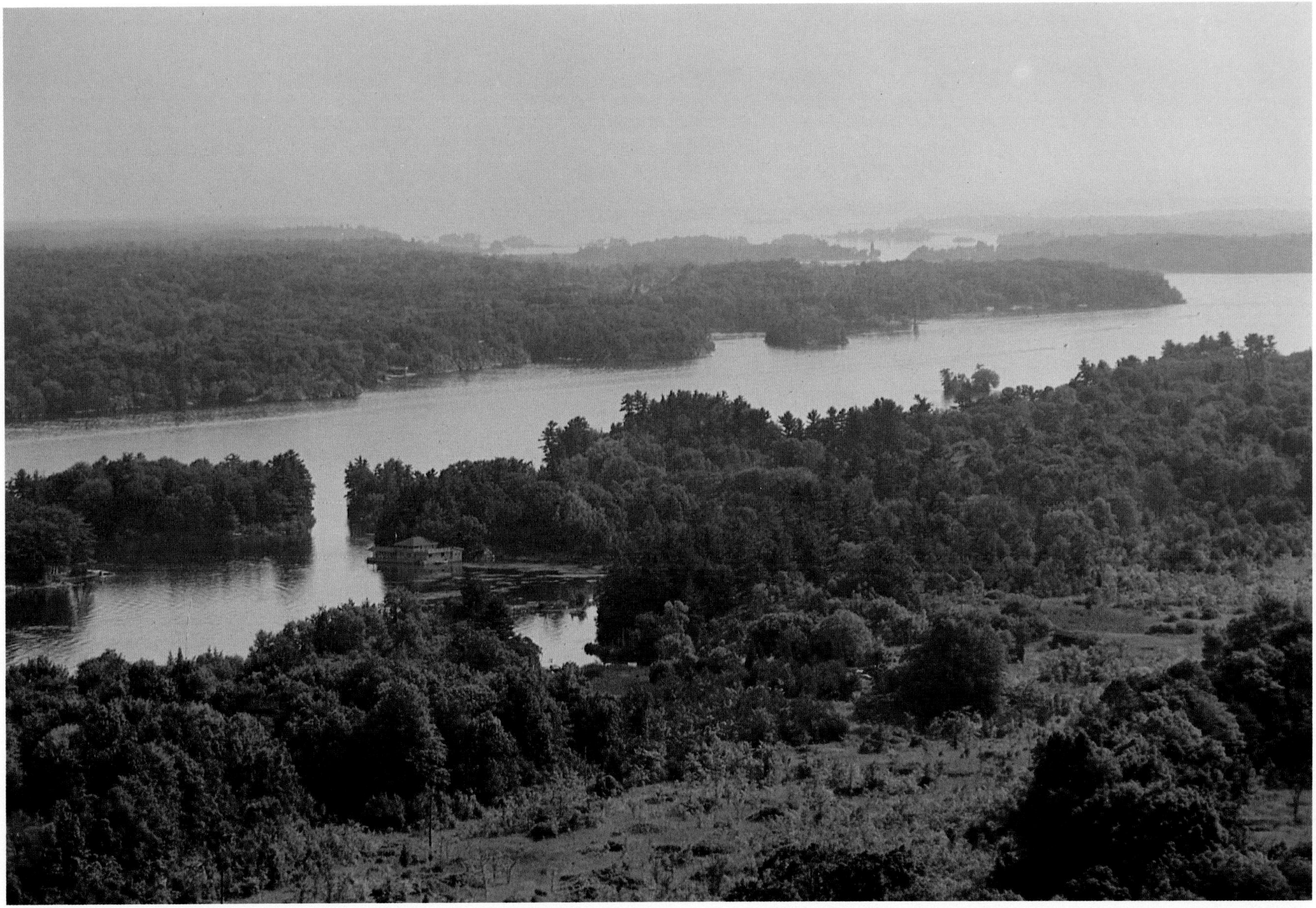

14 By Shelter Valley Road
15 St Lawrence Islands, near Ivylea

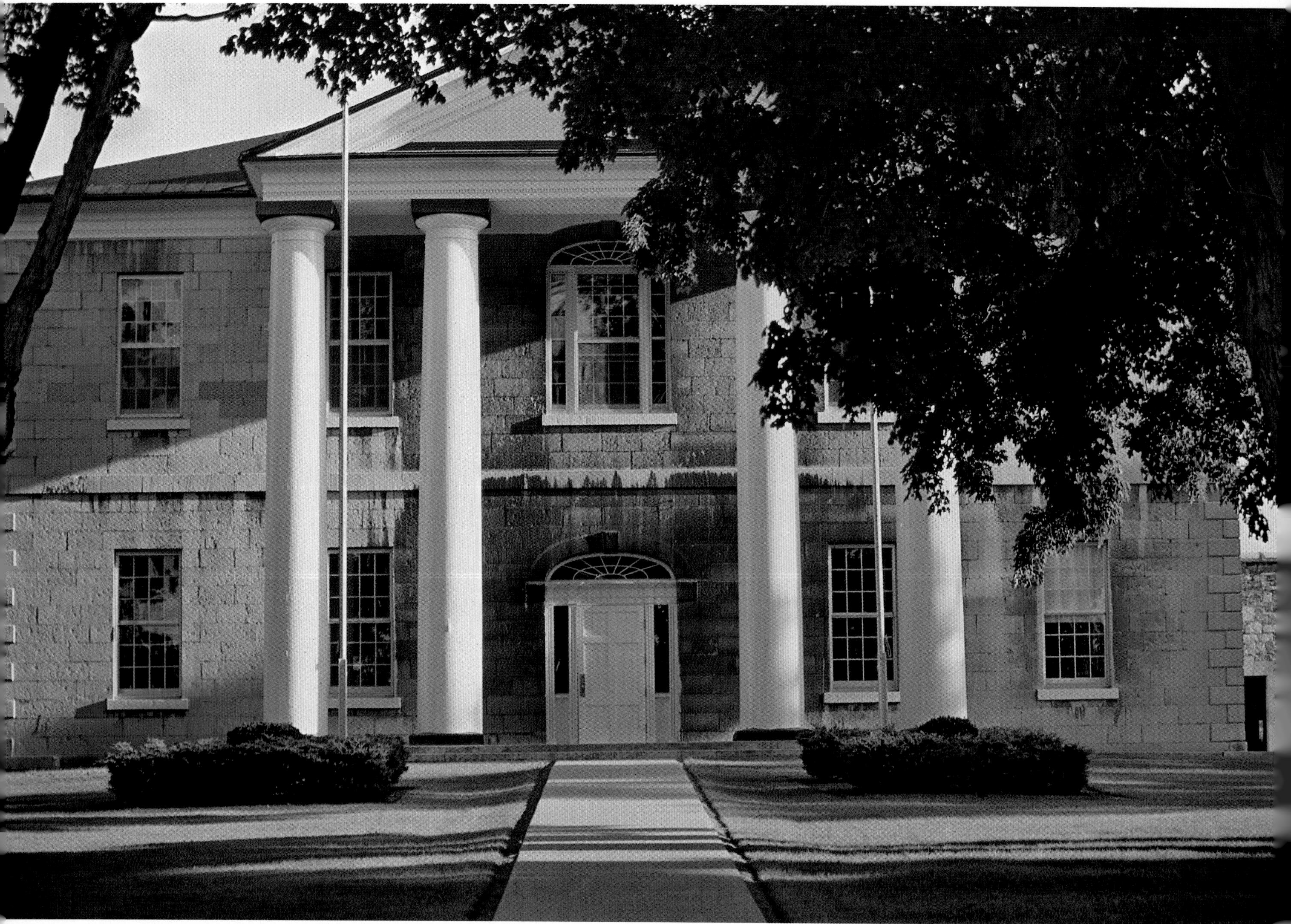

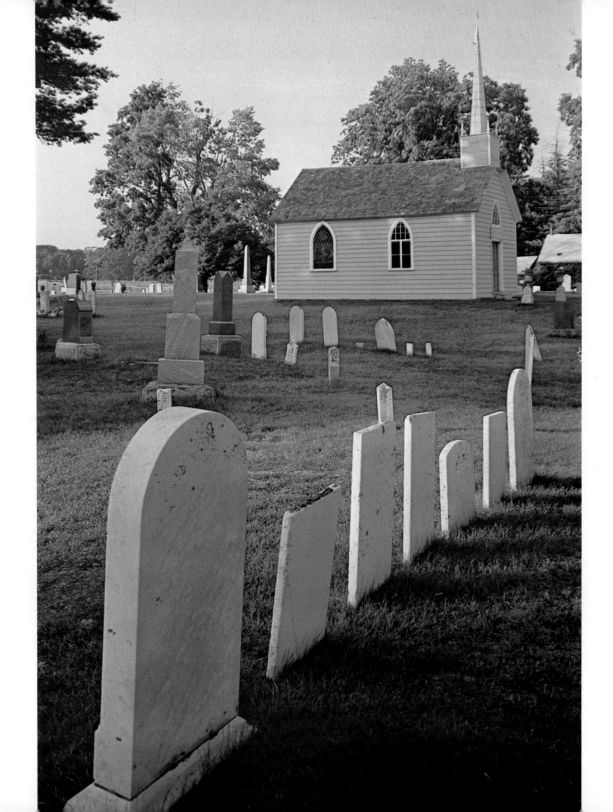

16 Courthouse, Picton
17 Blue Church, Maitland

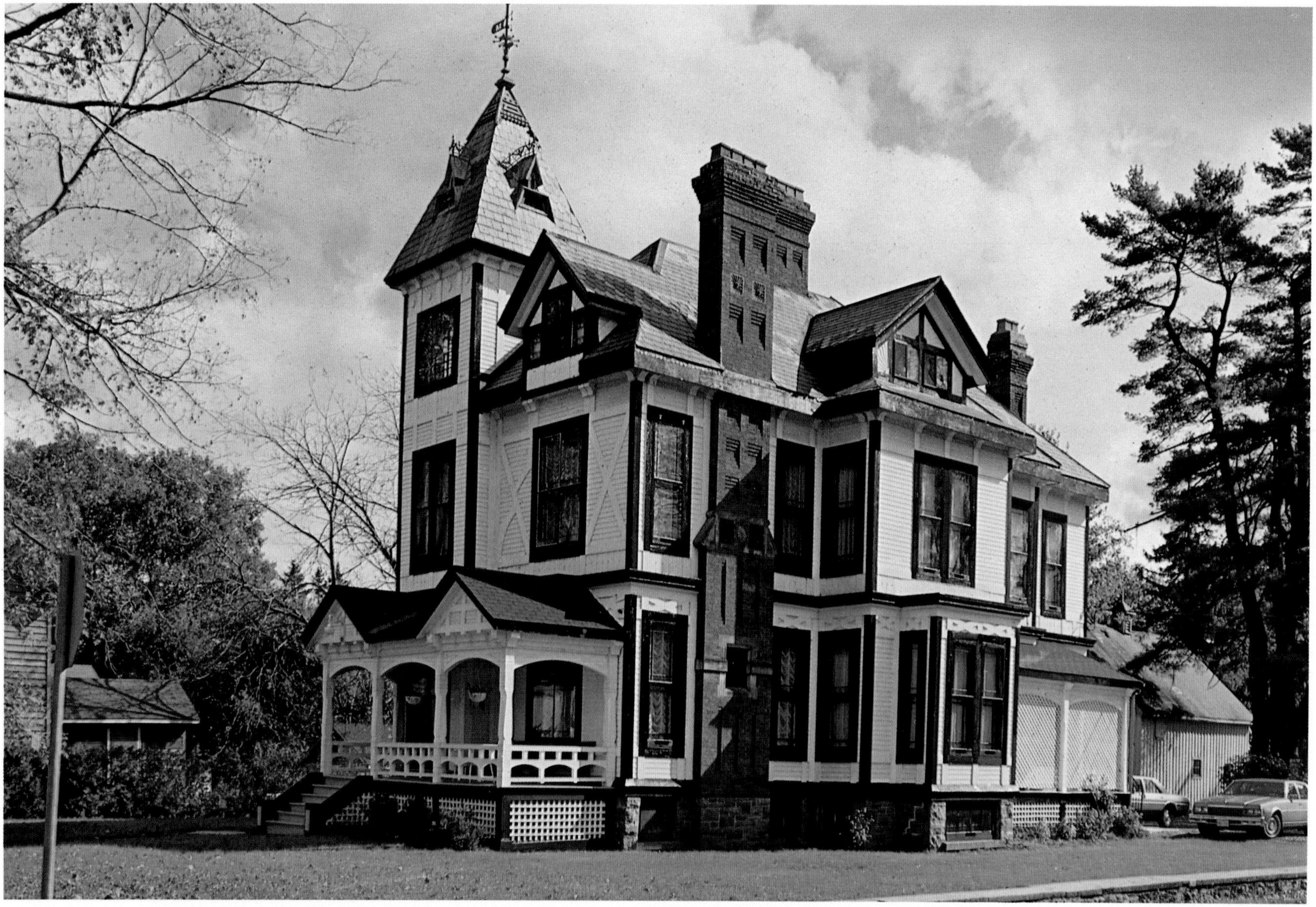

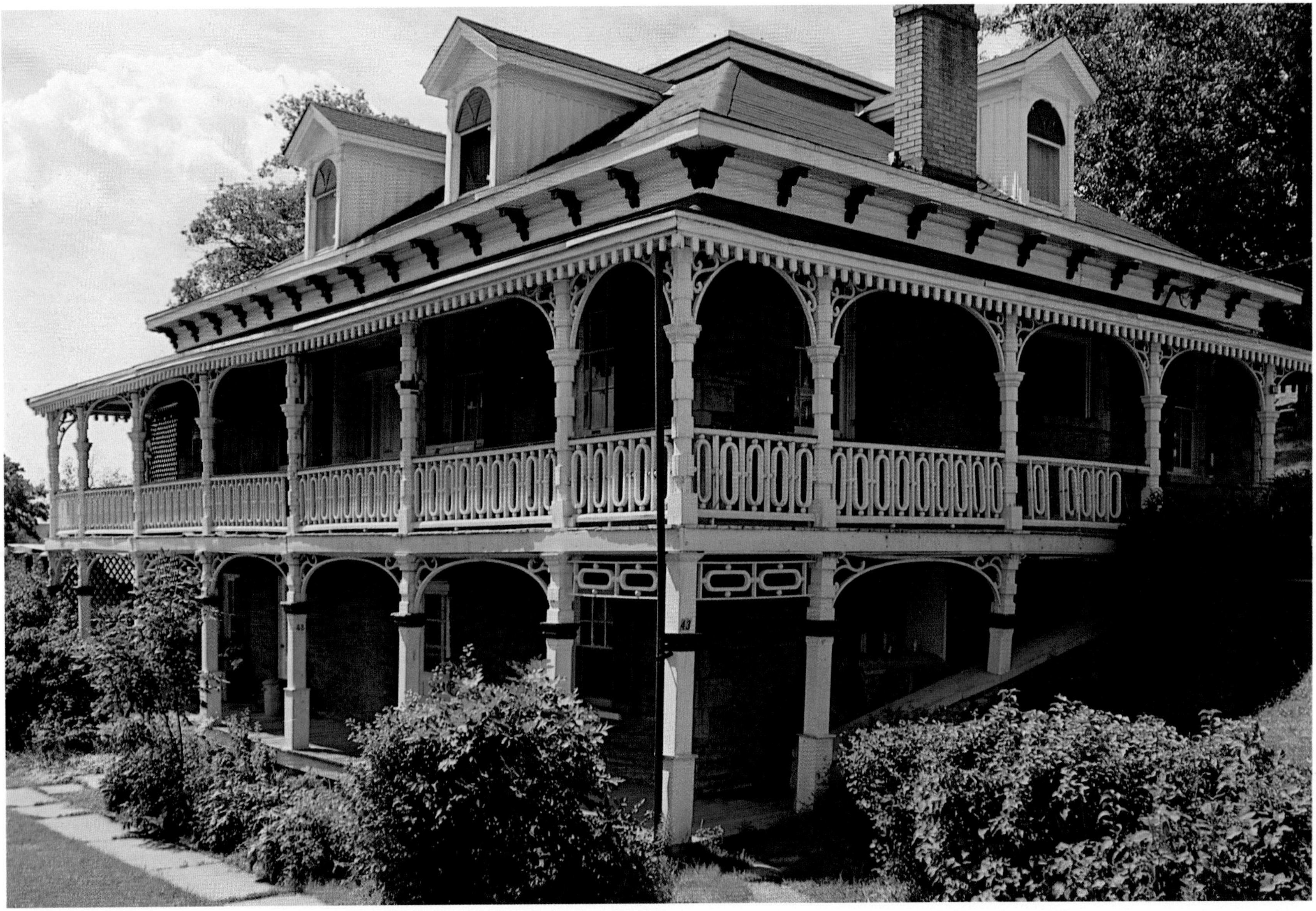

19 Belleville

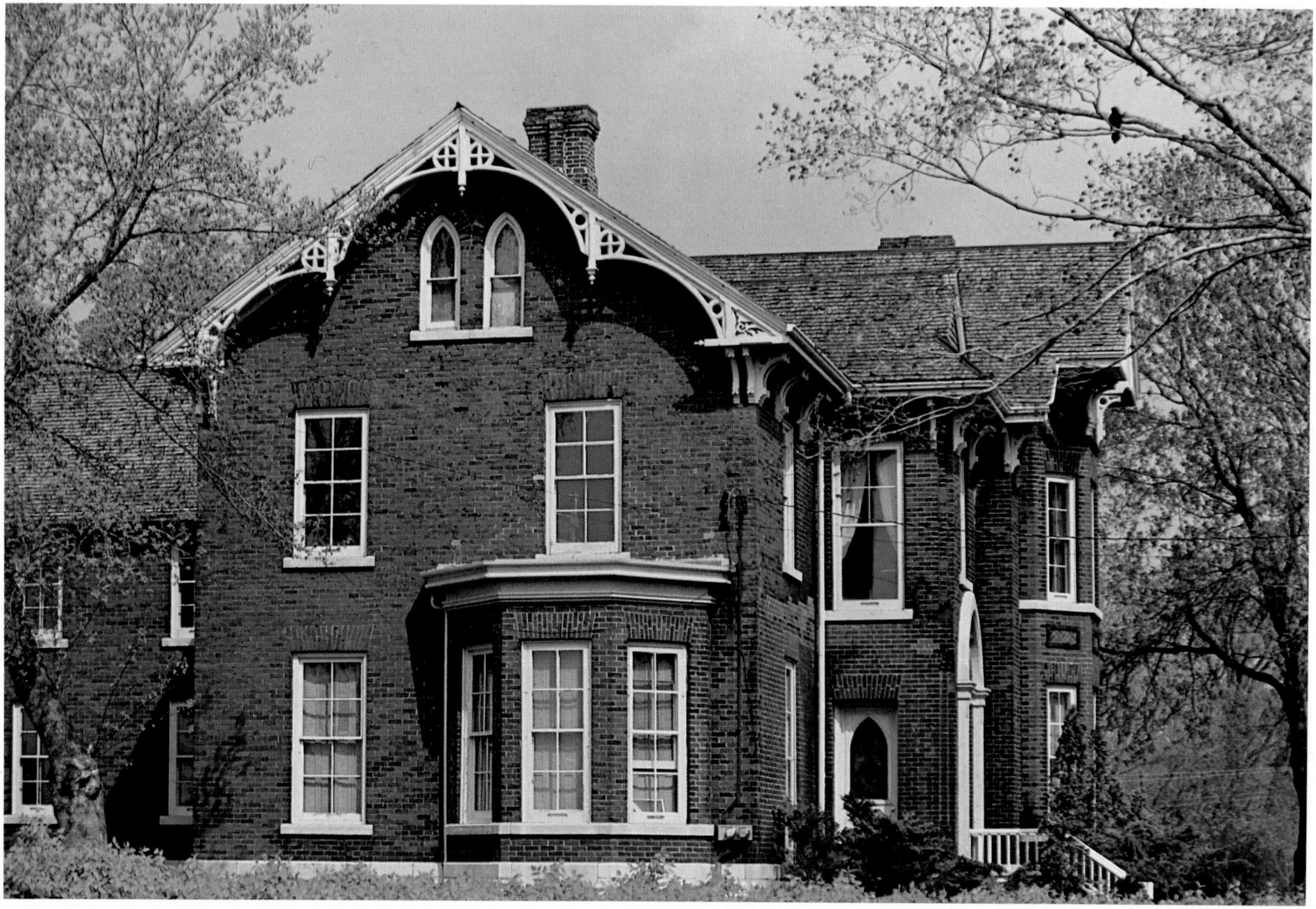

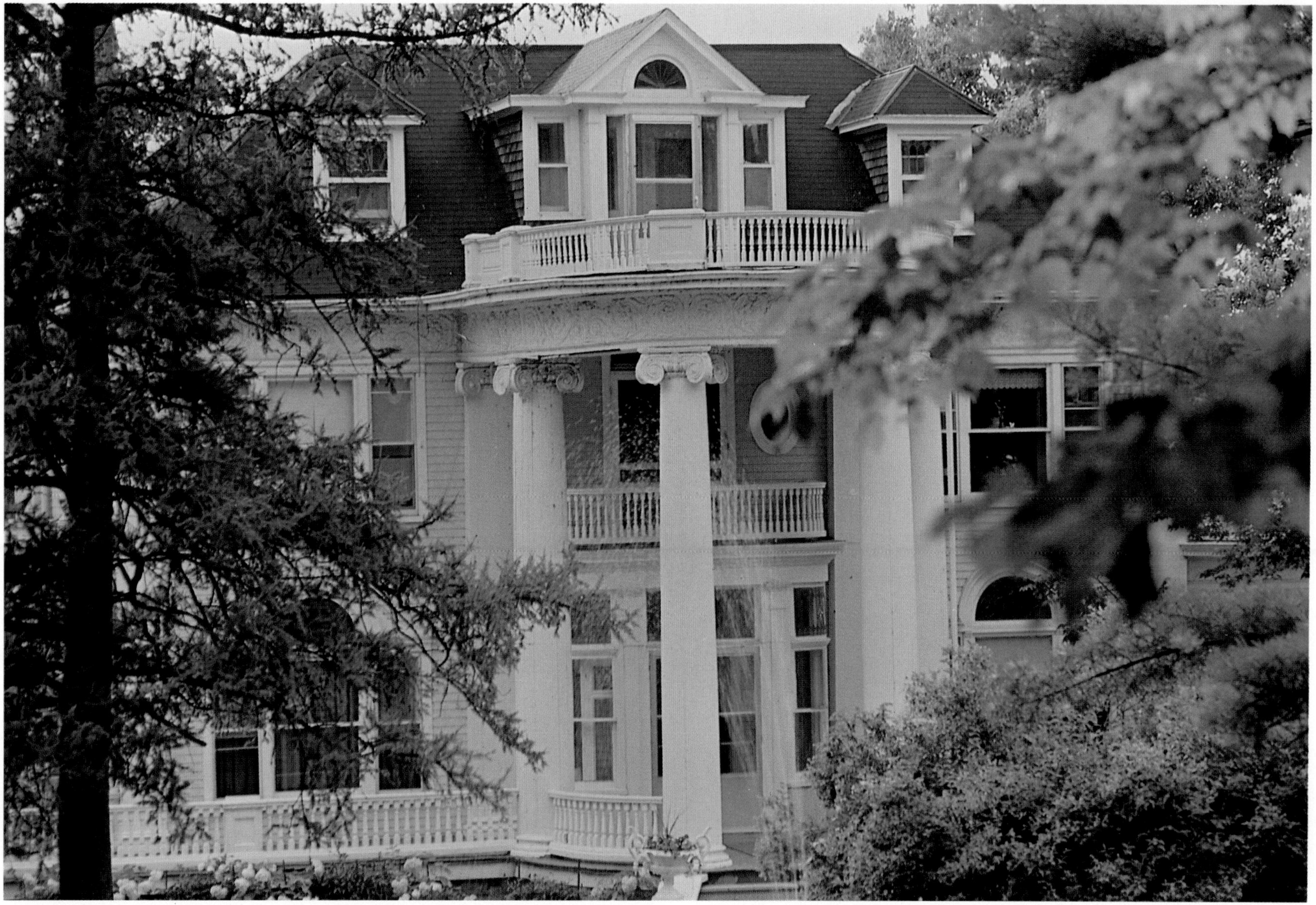

21 Prince Edward County Club, Picton

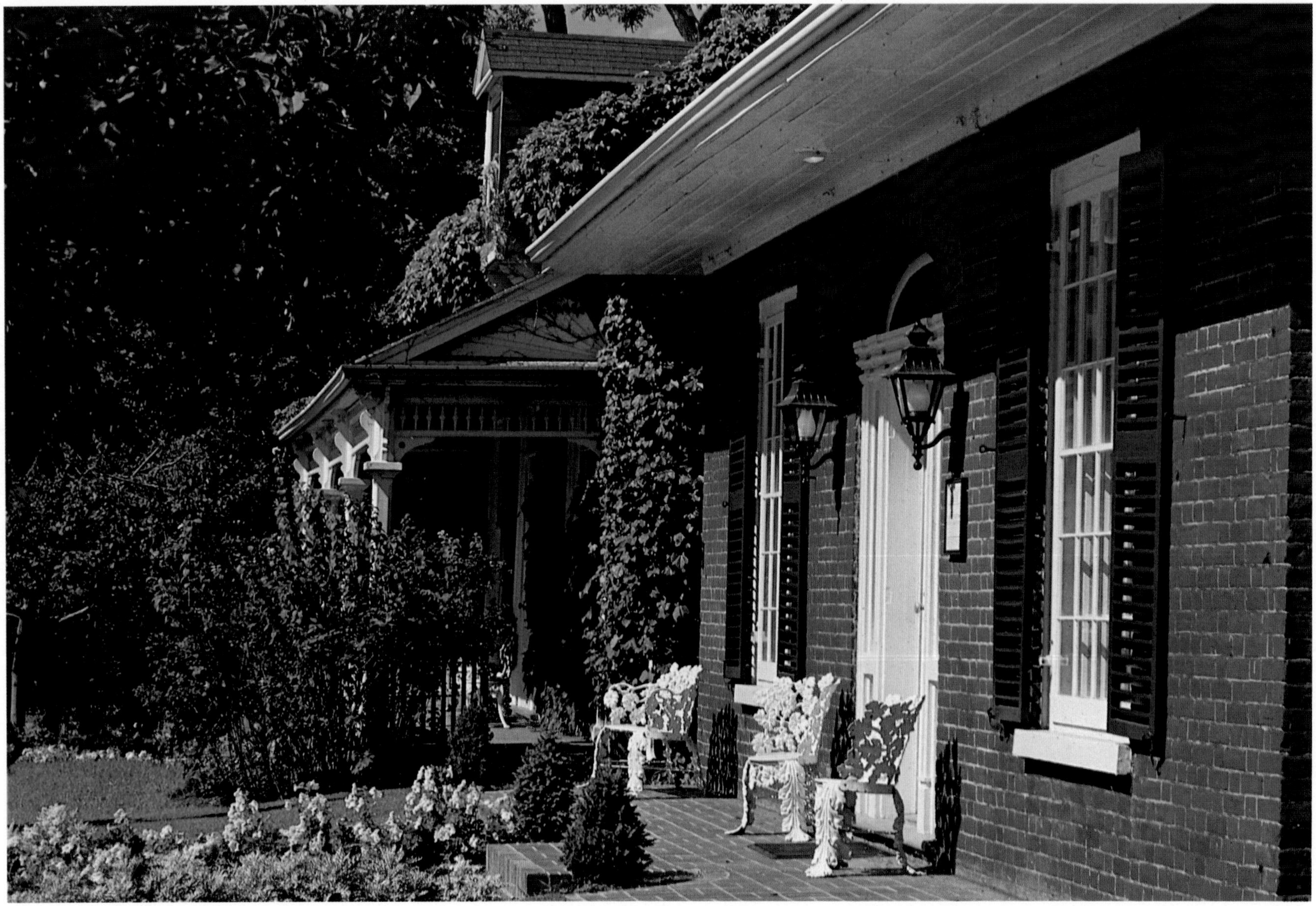

22 Marie Dressler House, Cobourg

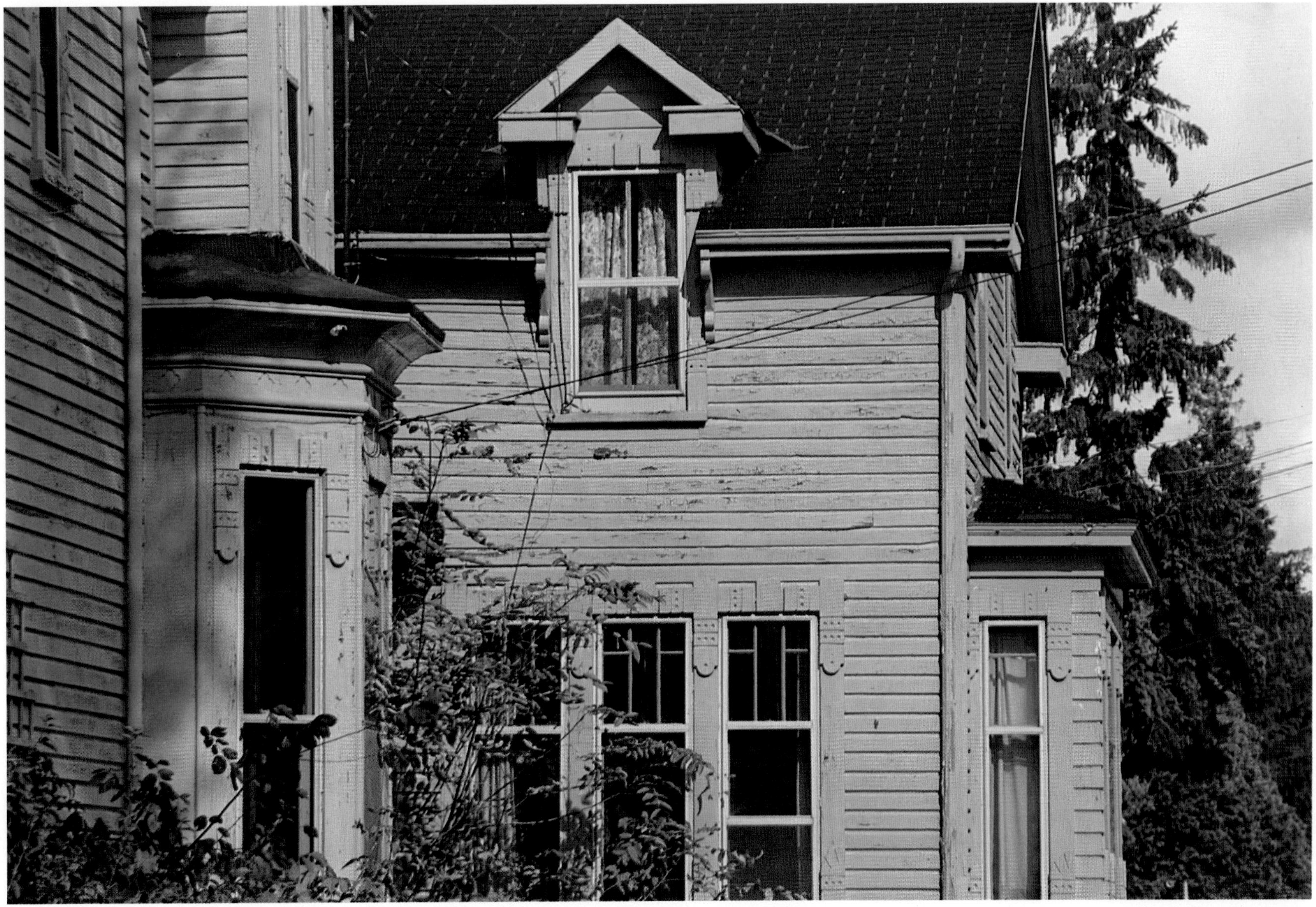

23 Gananoque

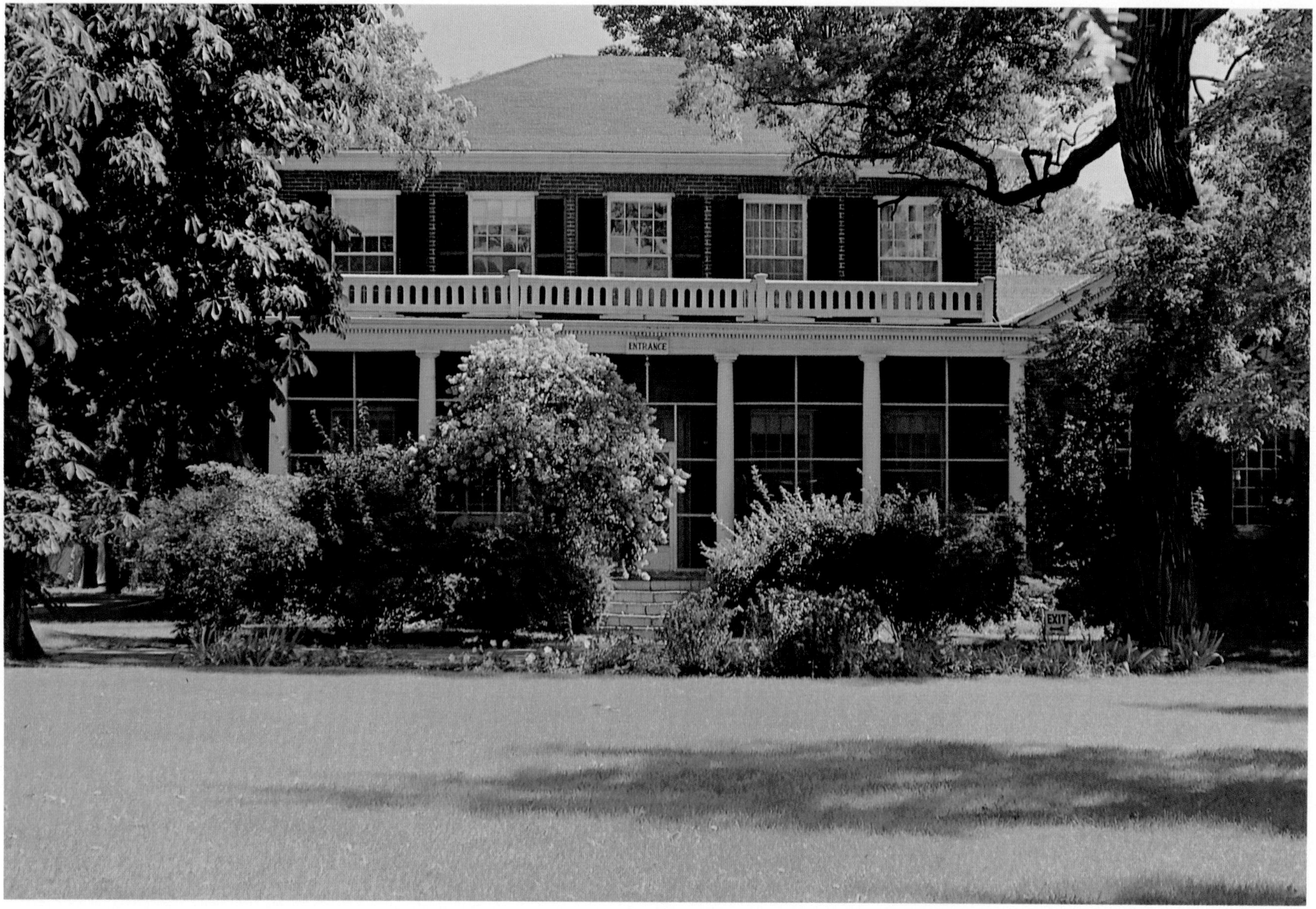
ENTRANCE
EXIT

24 Cobourg
25 Seymour Township

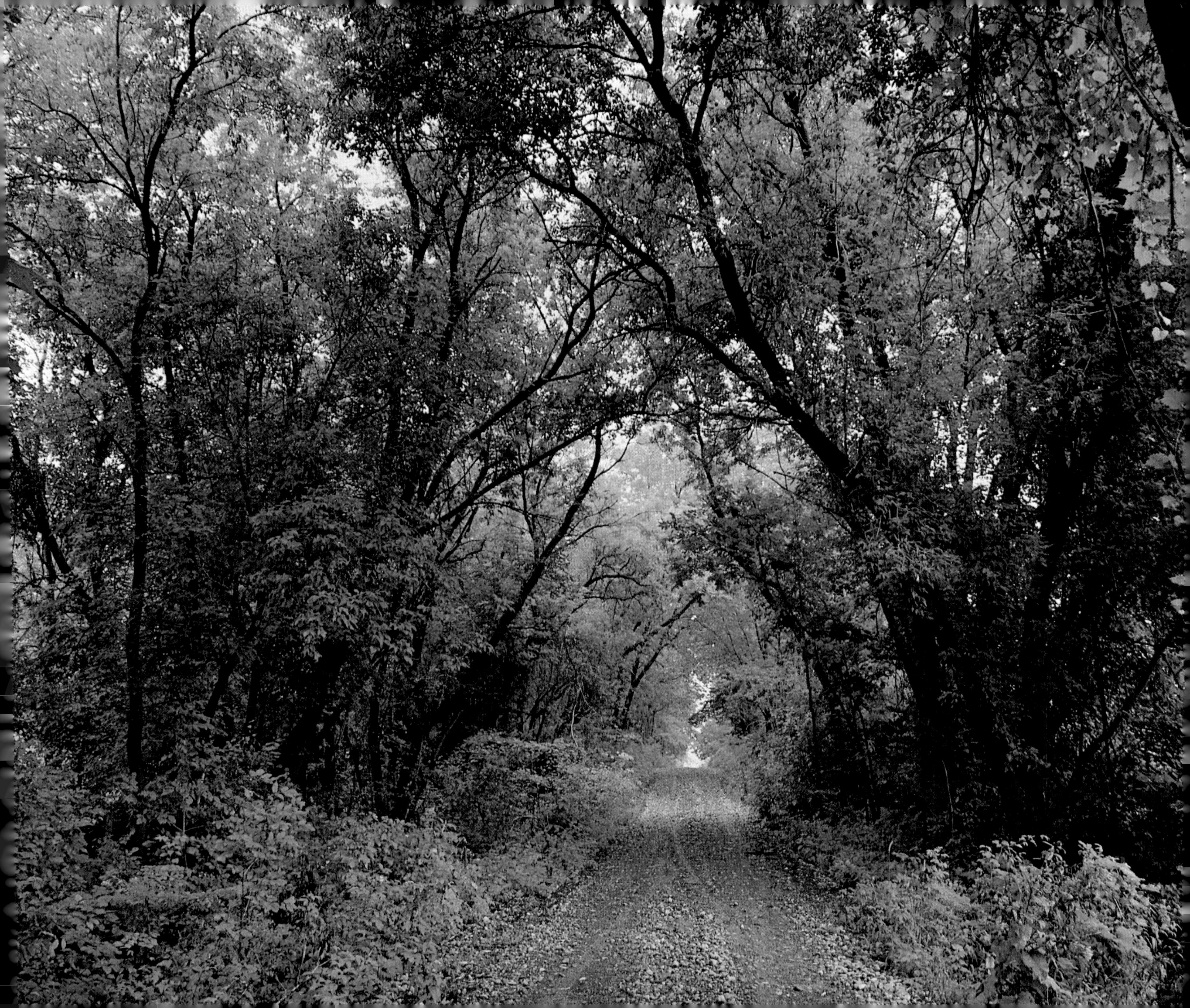

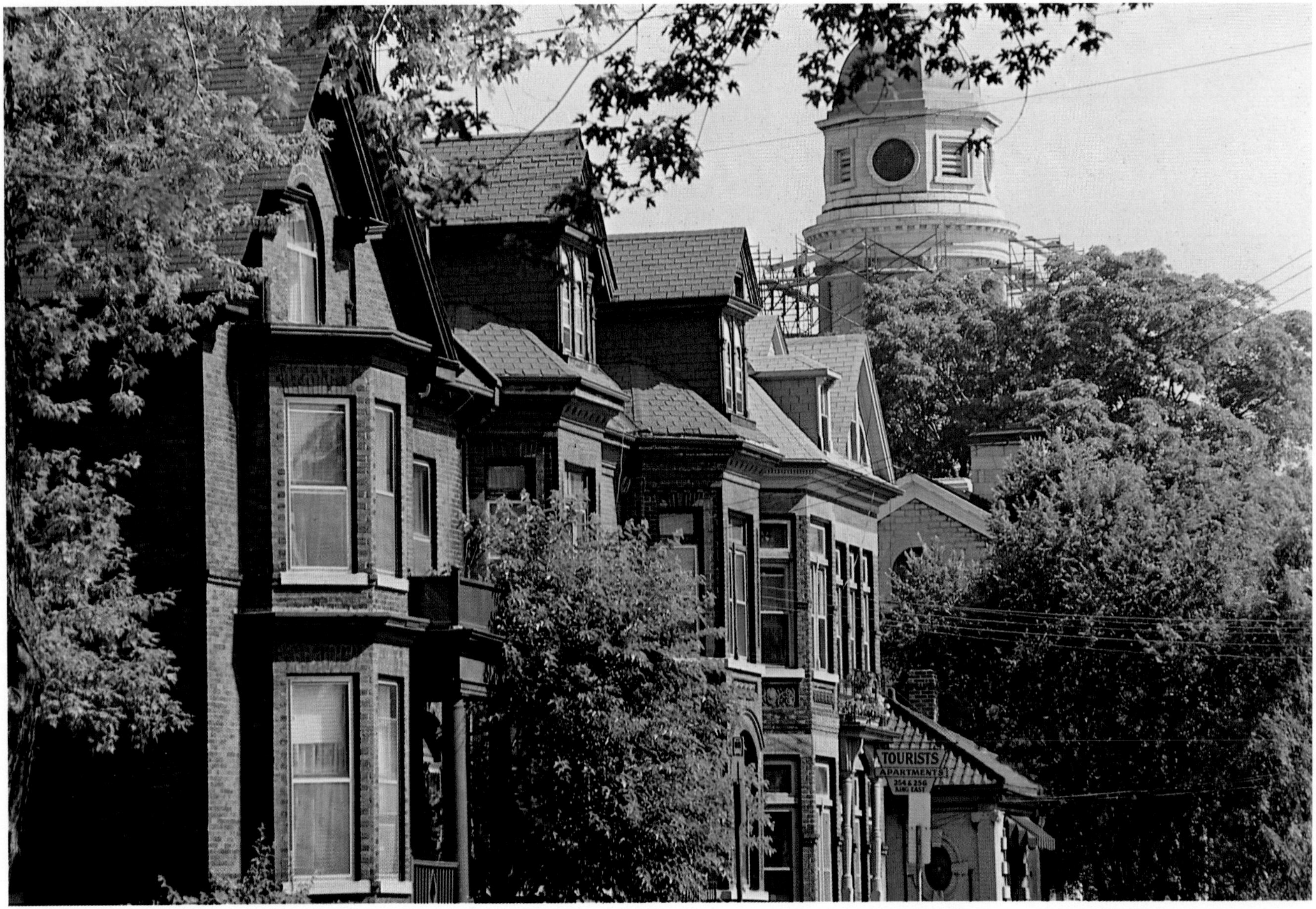
TOURISTS
APARTMENTS
254 & 256
KING EAST

26 Kingston
27 Gananoque

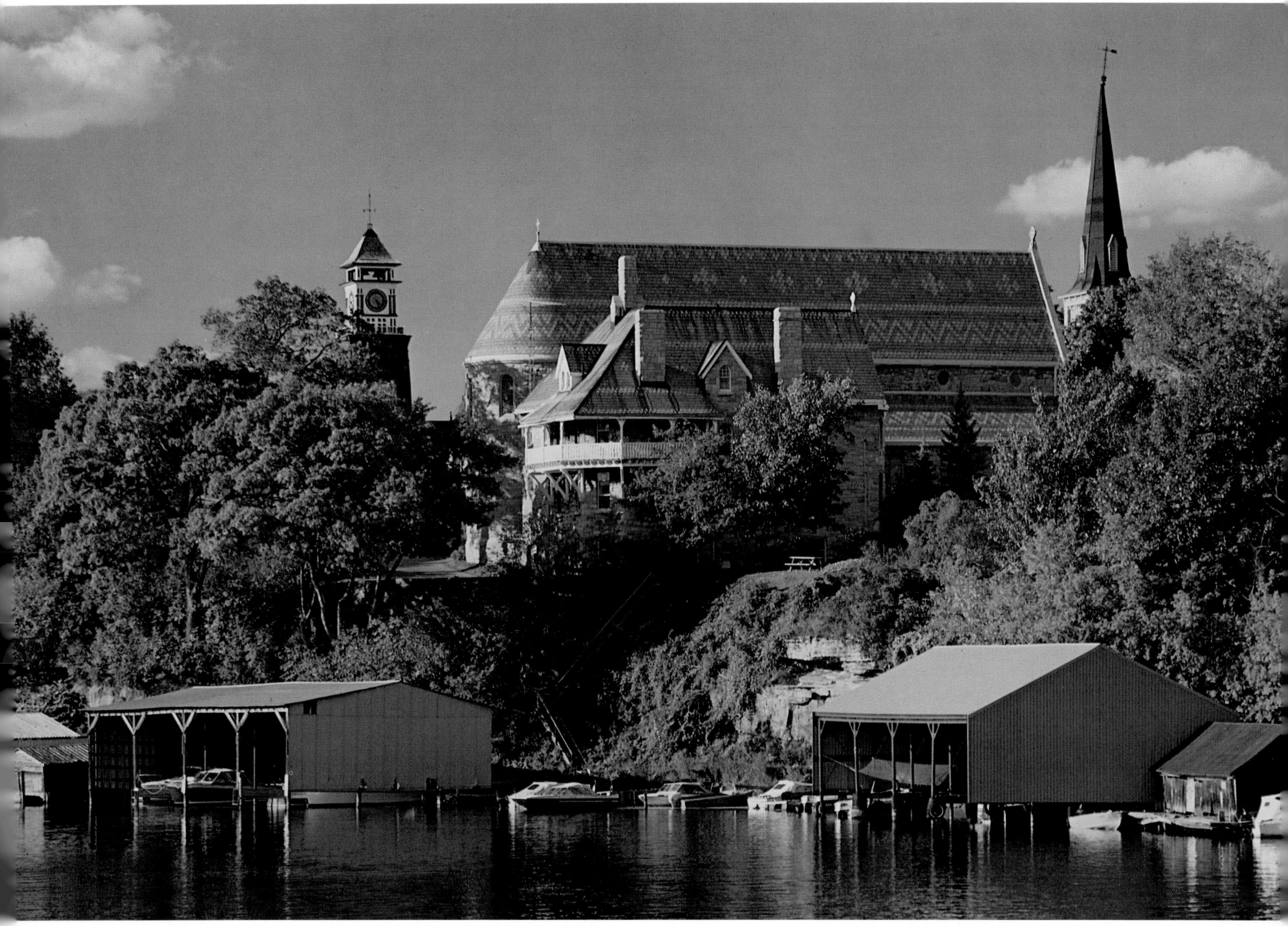

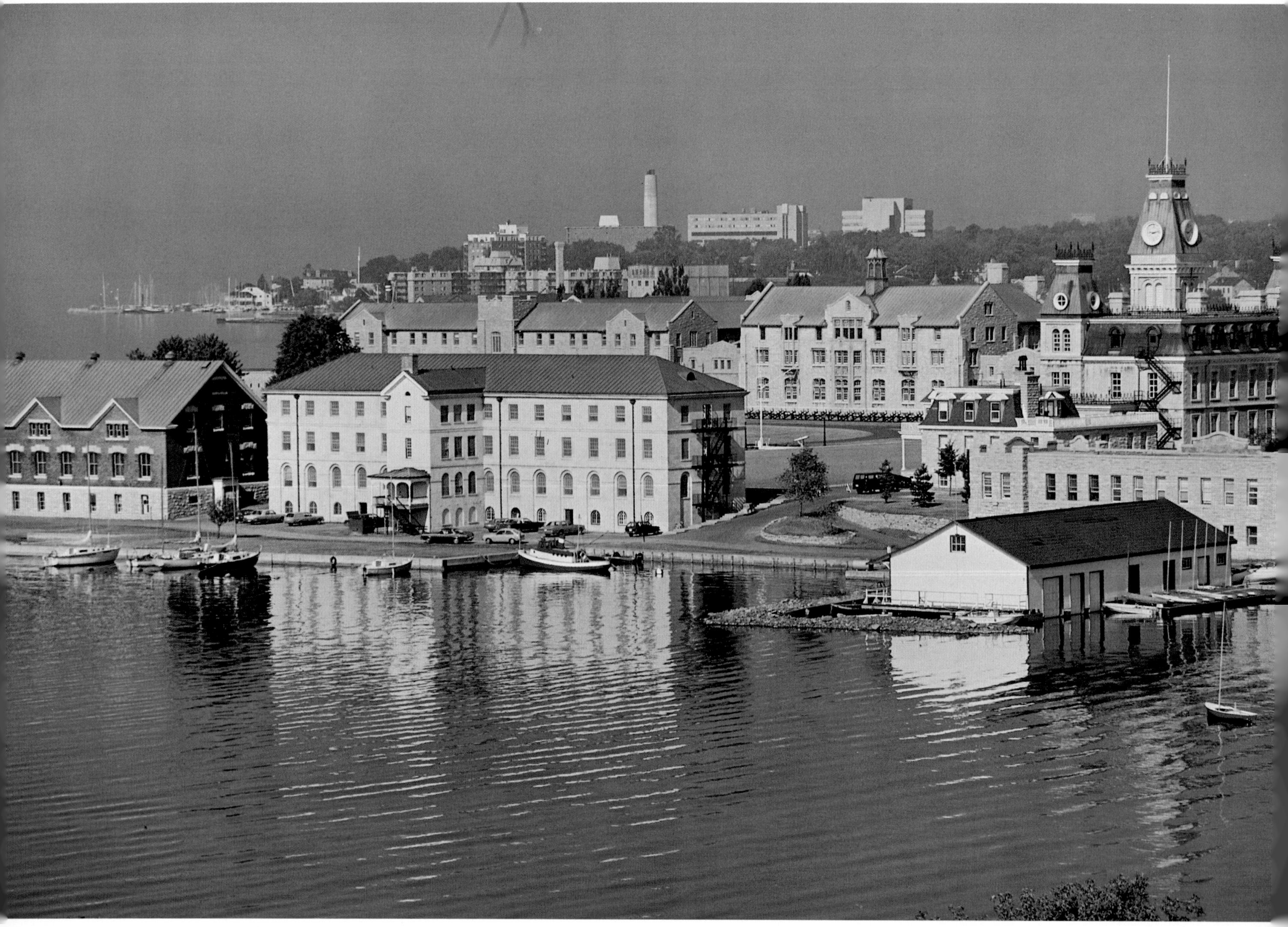

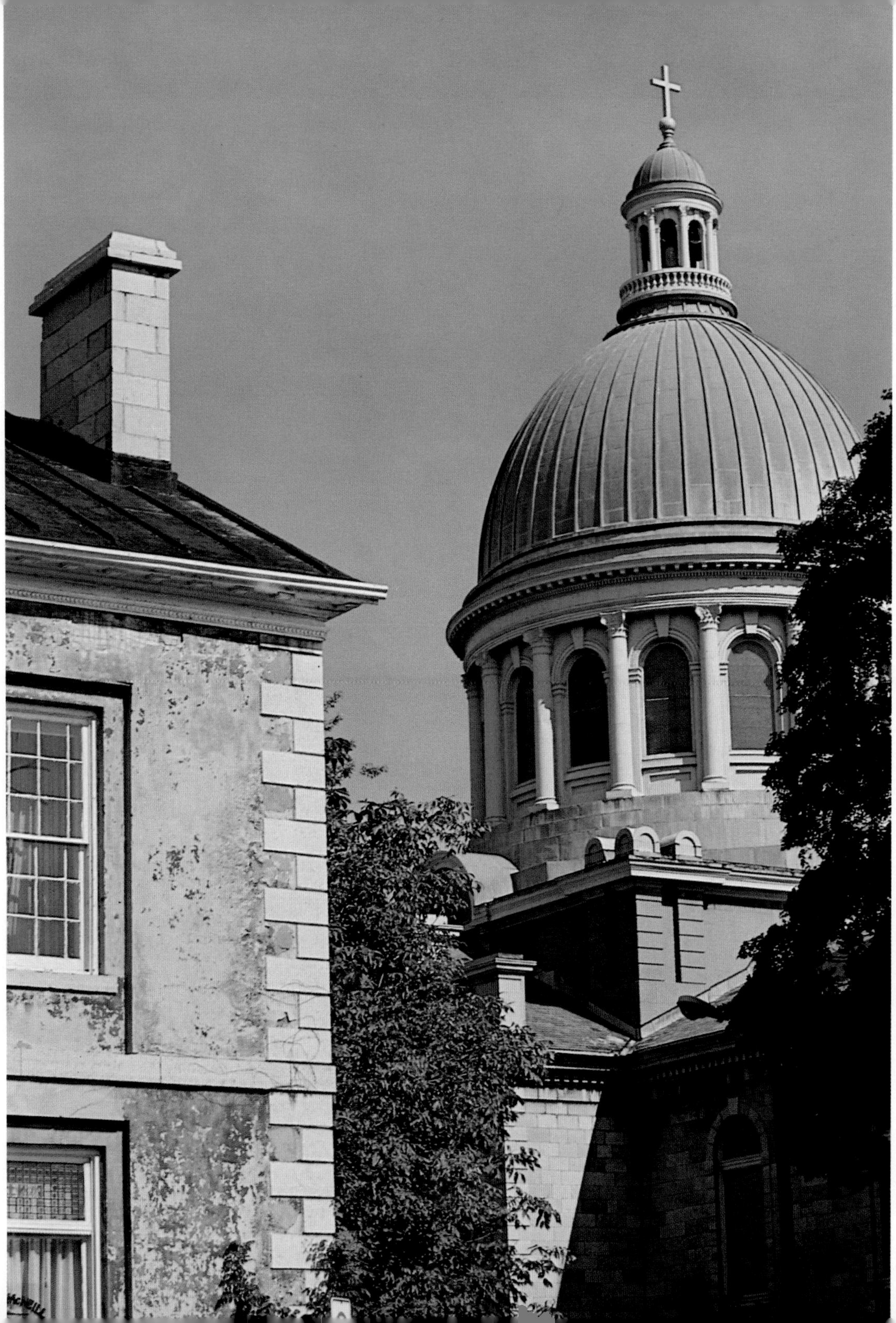

28 Royal Military College, Kingston
29 Kingston

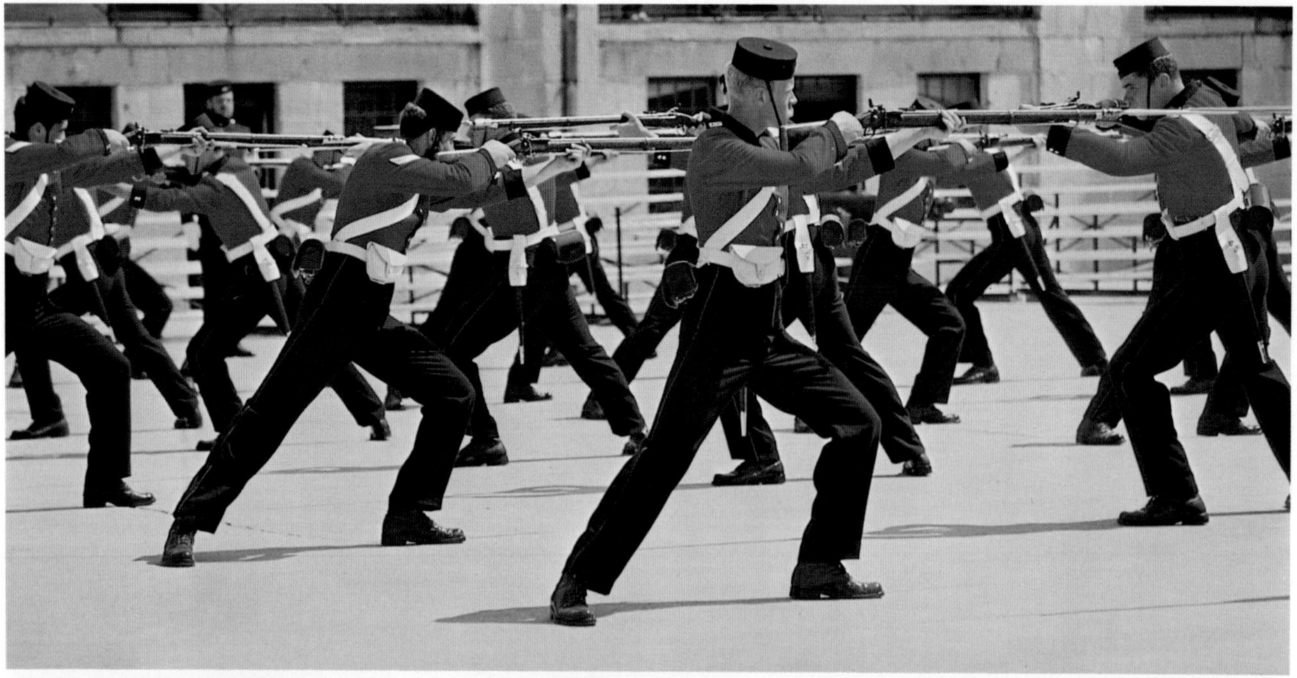

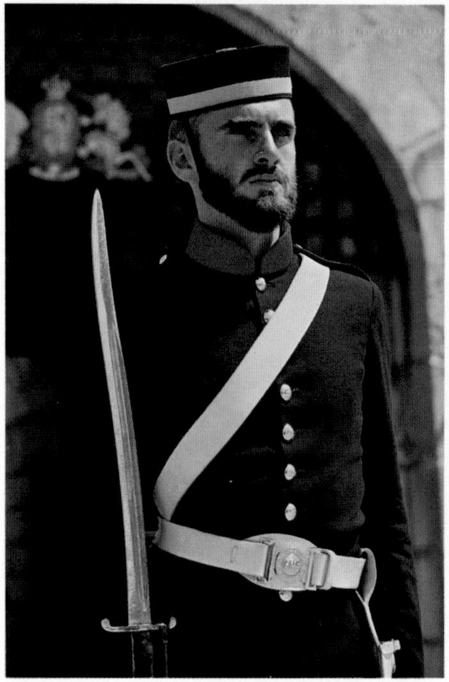

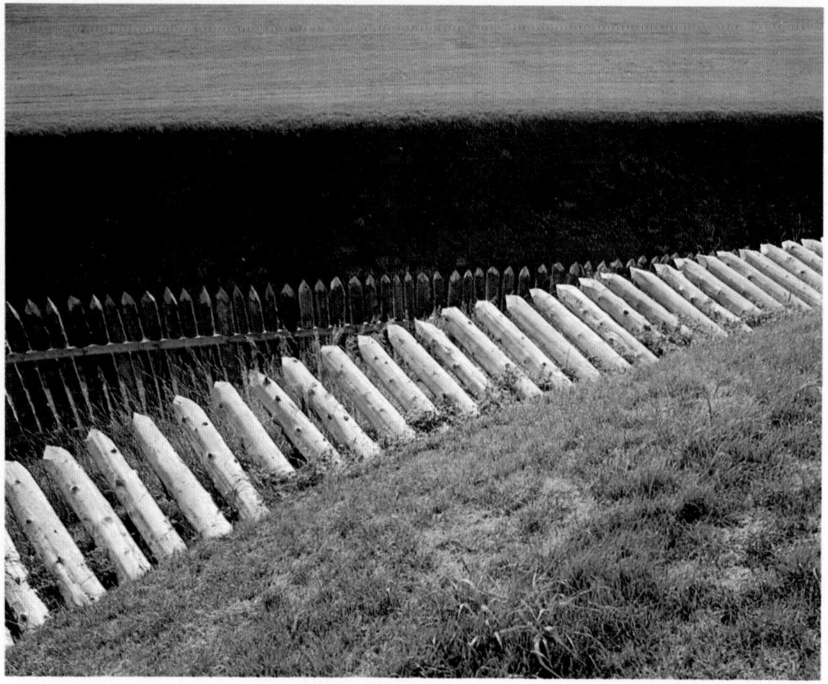

30 (a) Fort Henry, Kingston
30 (b) Fort Henry, Kingston
30 (c) Fort Wellington, Prescott
31 Fort Henry, Kingston

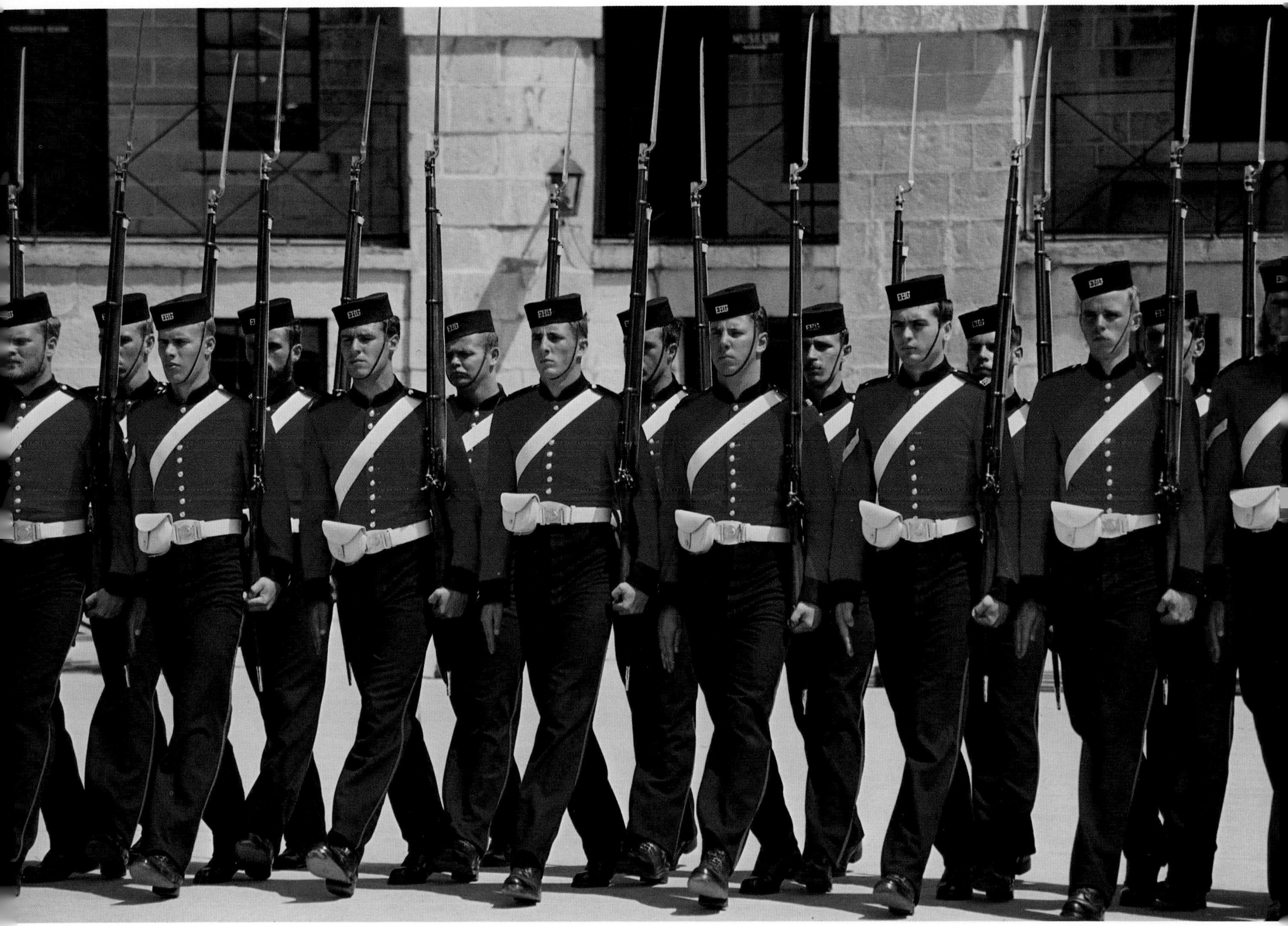

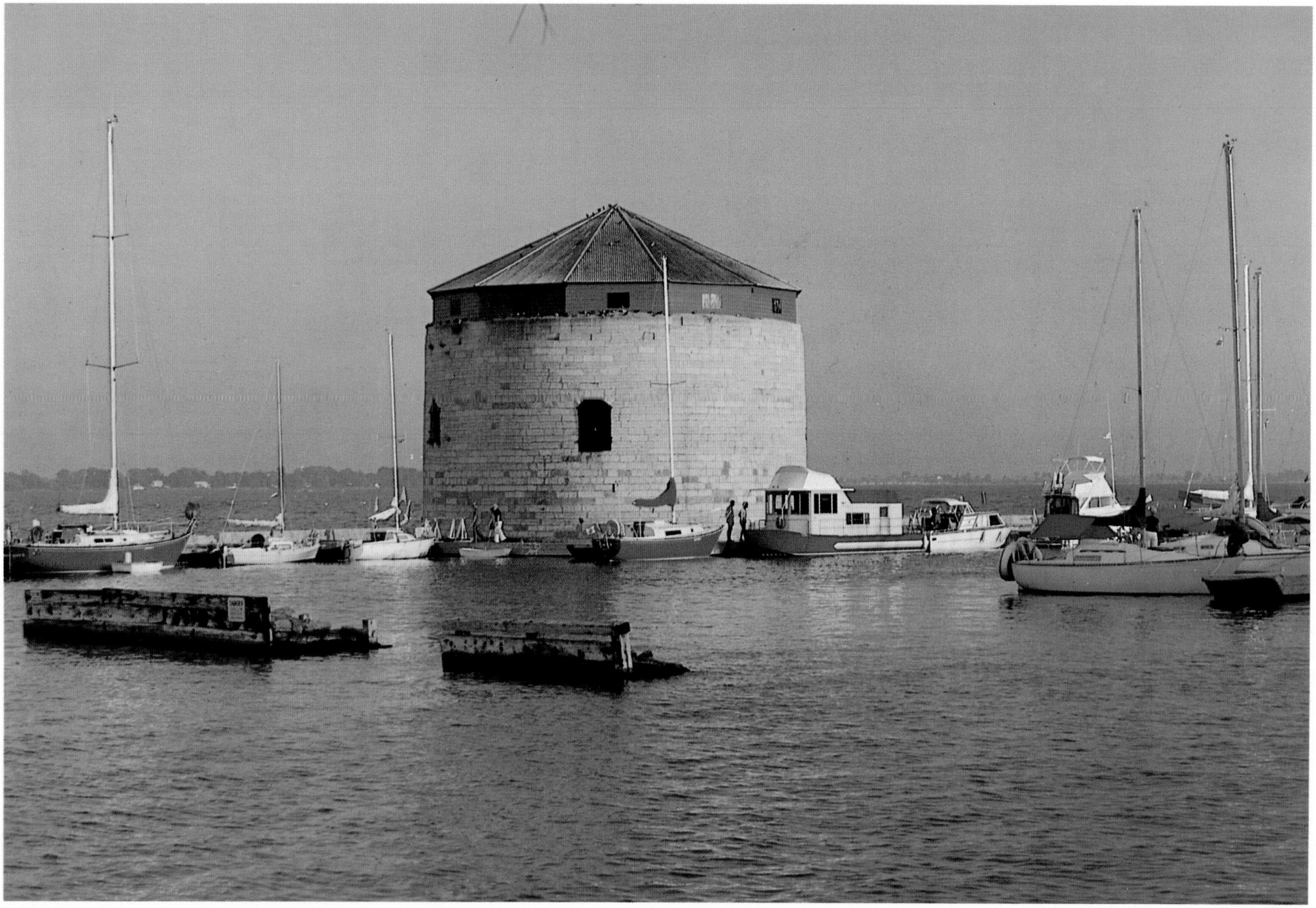

32 Shoal Tower, Kingston

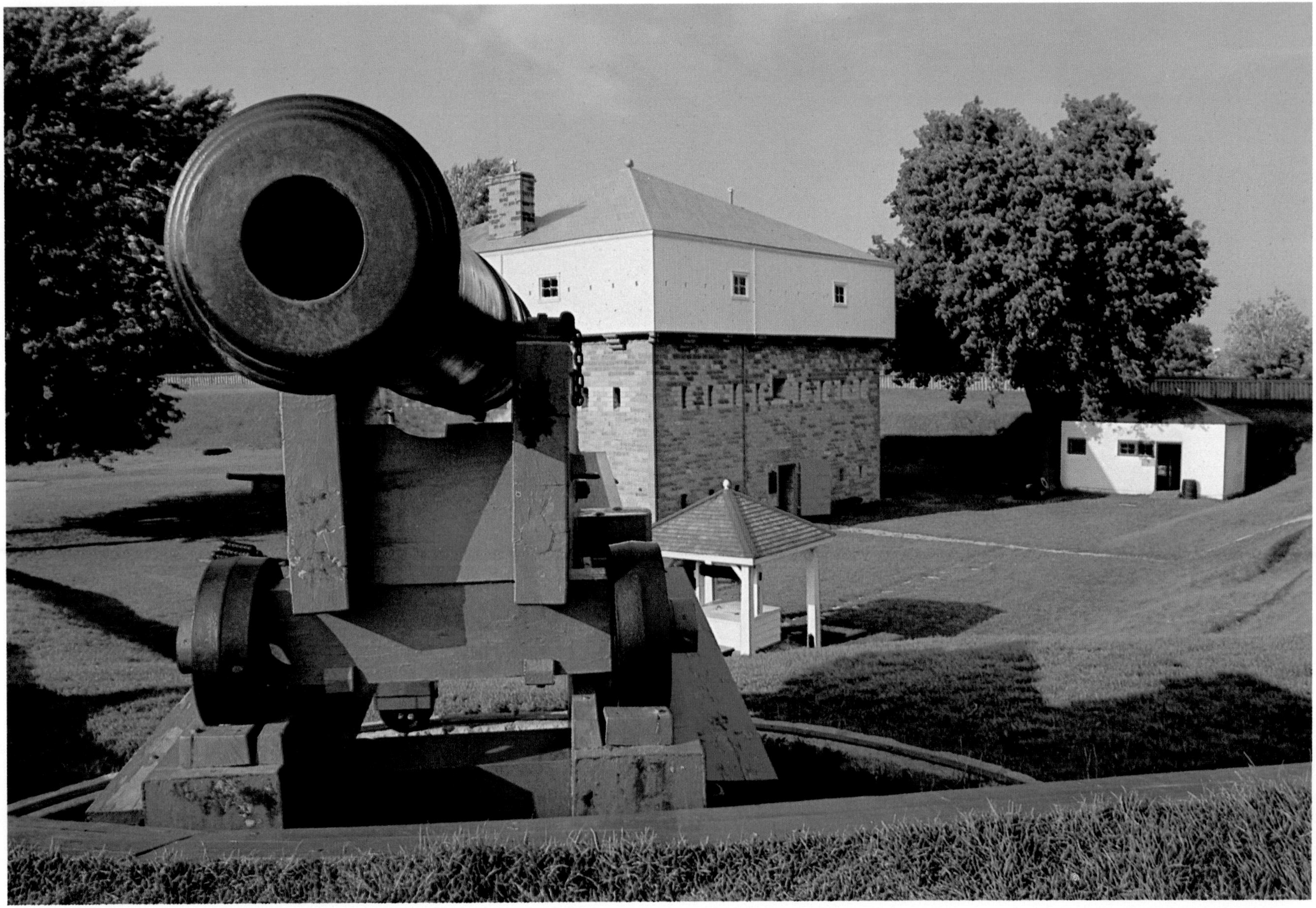

33 Fort Wellington, Prescott

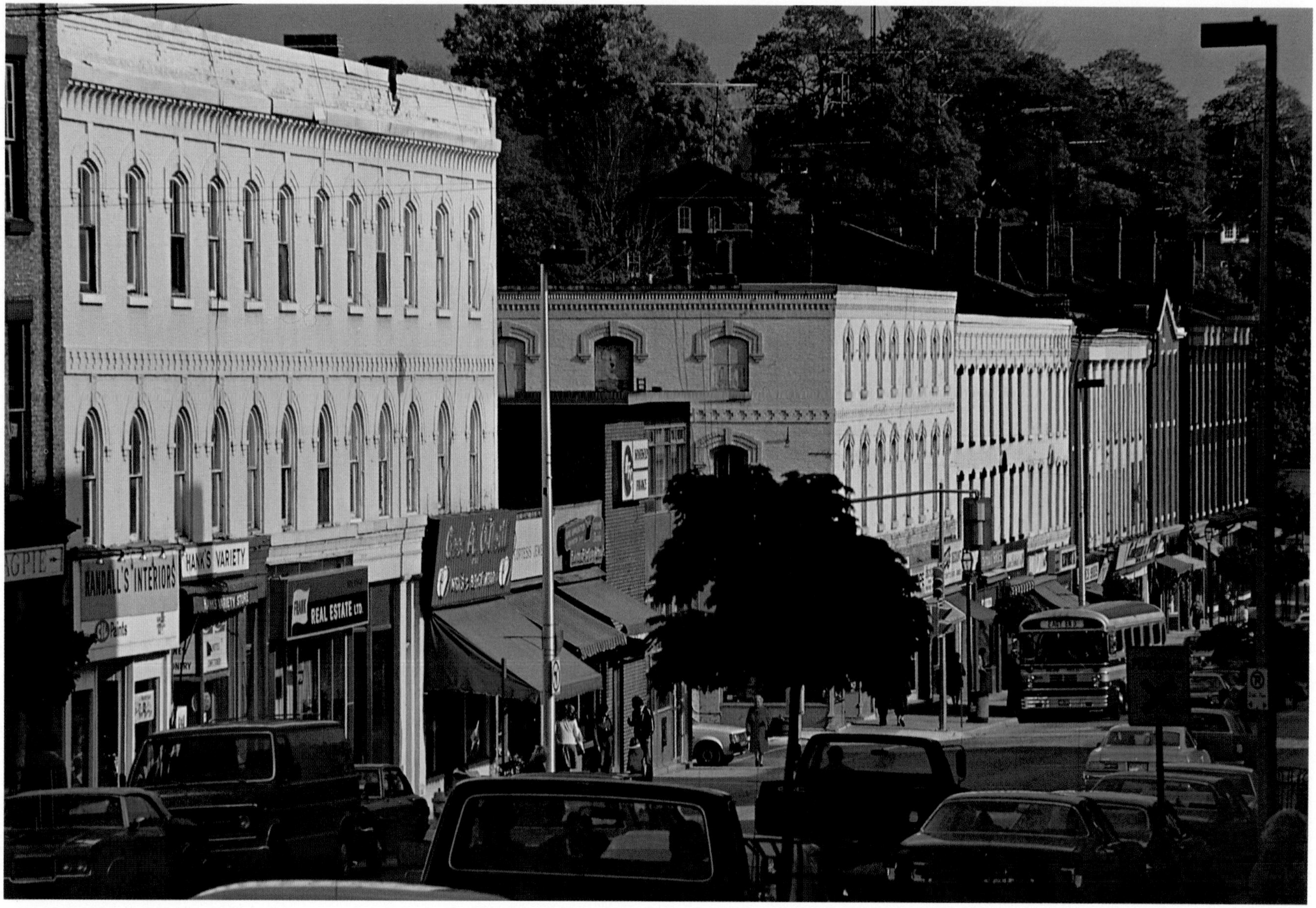
RANDALL'S INTERIORS
HANK'S VARIETY
REAL ESTATE LTD.

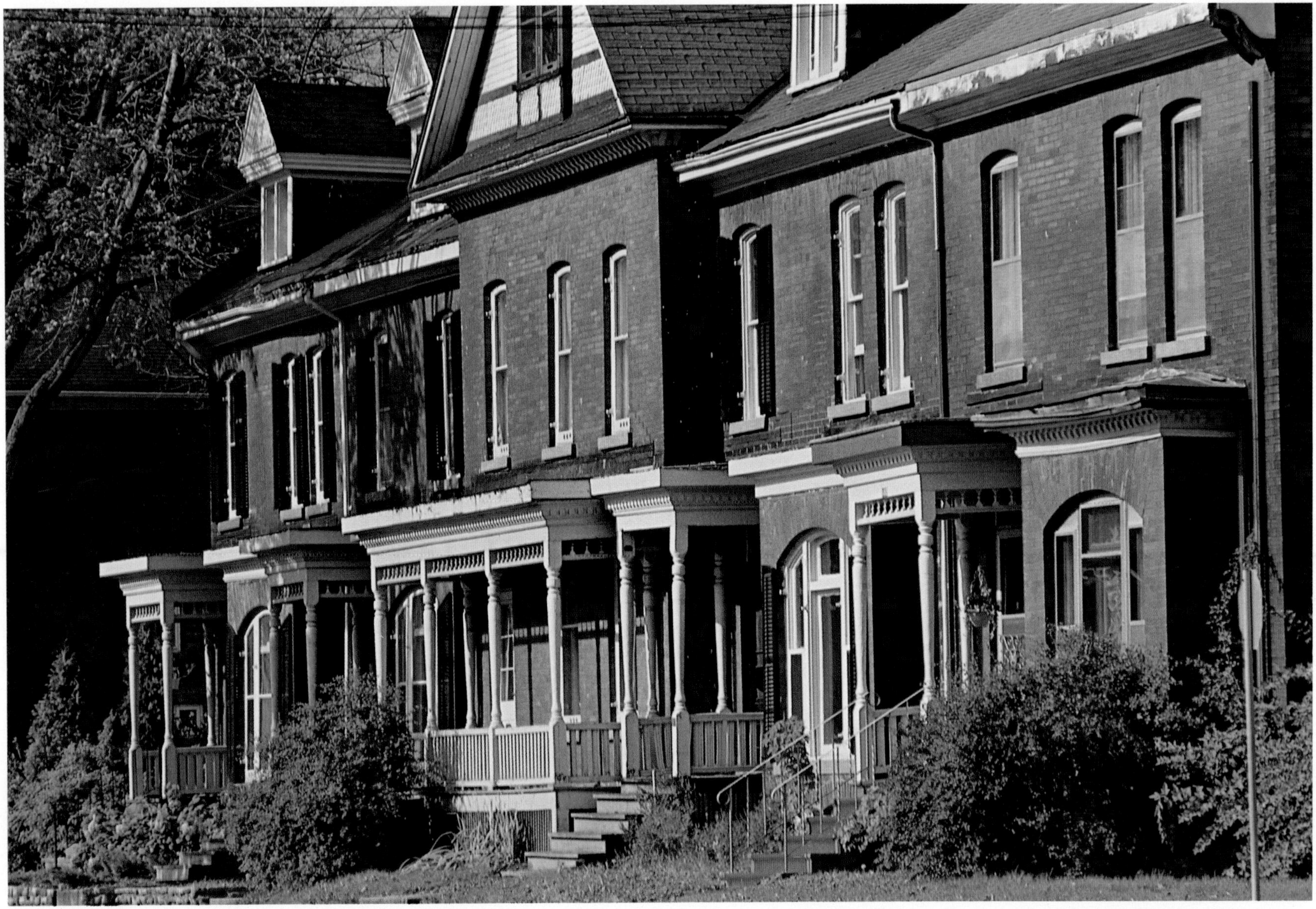

35 Brockville

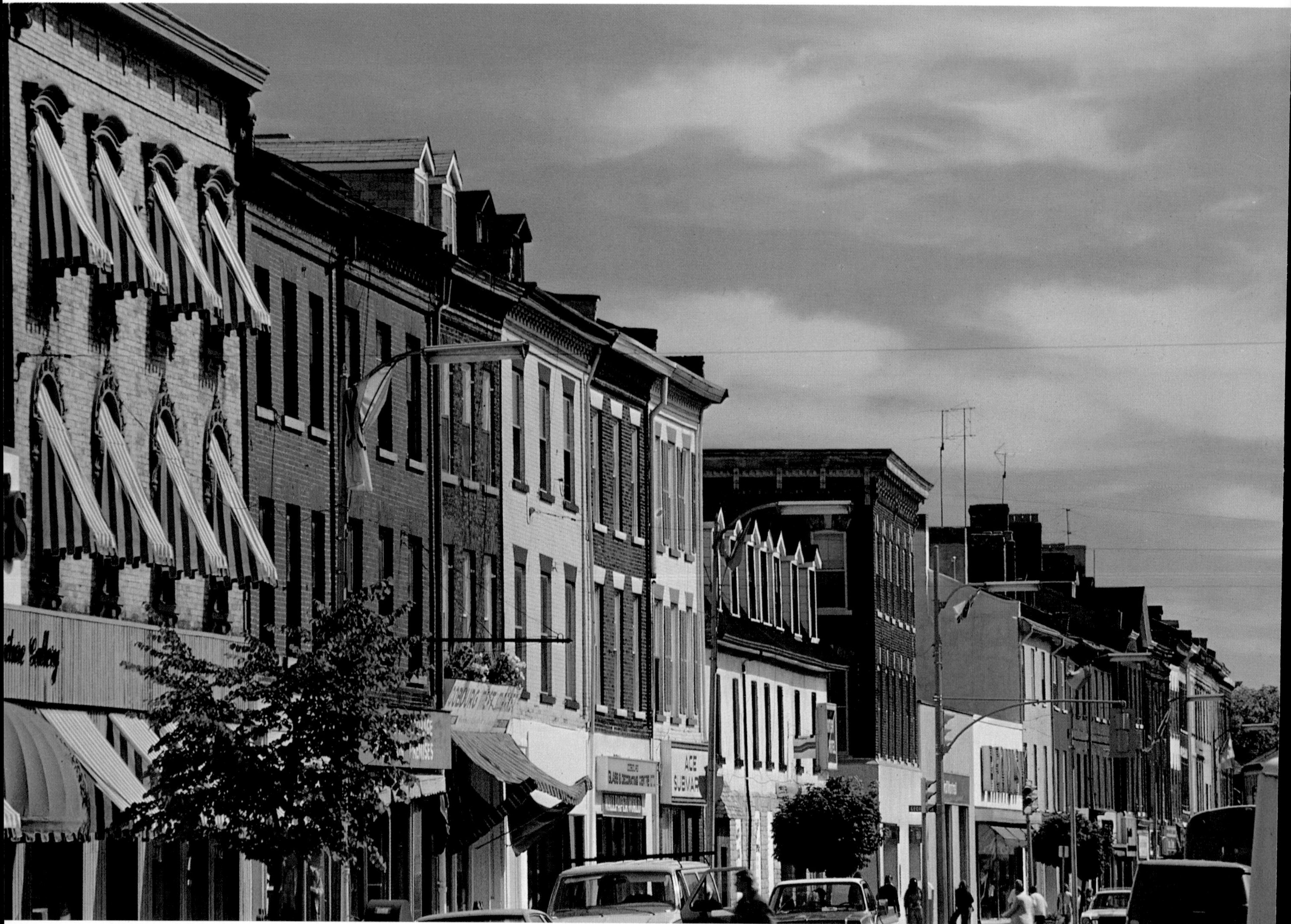
ACE

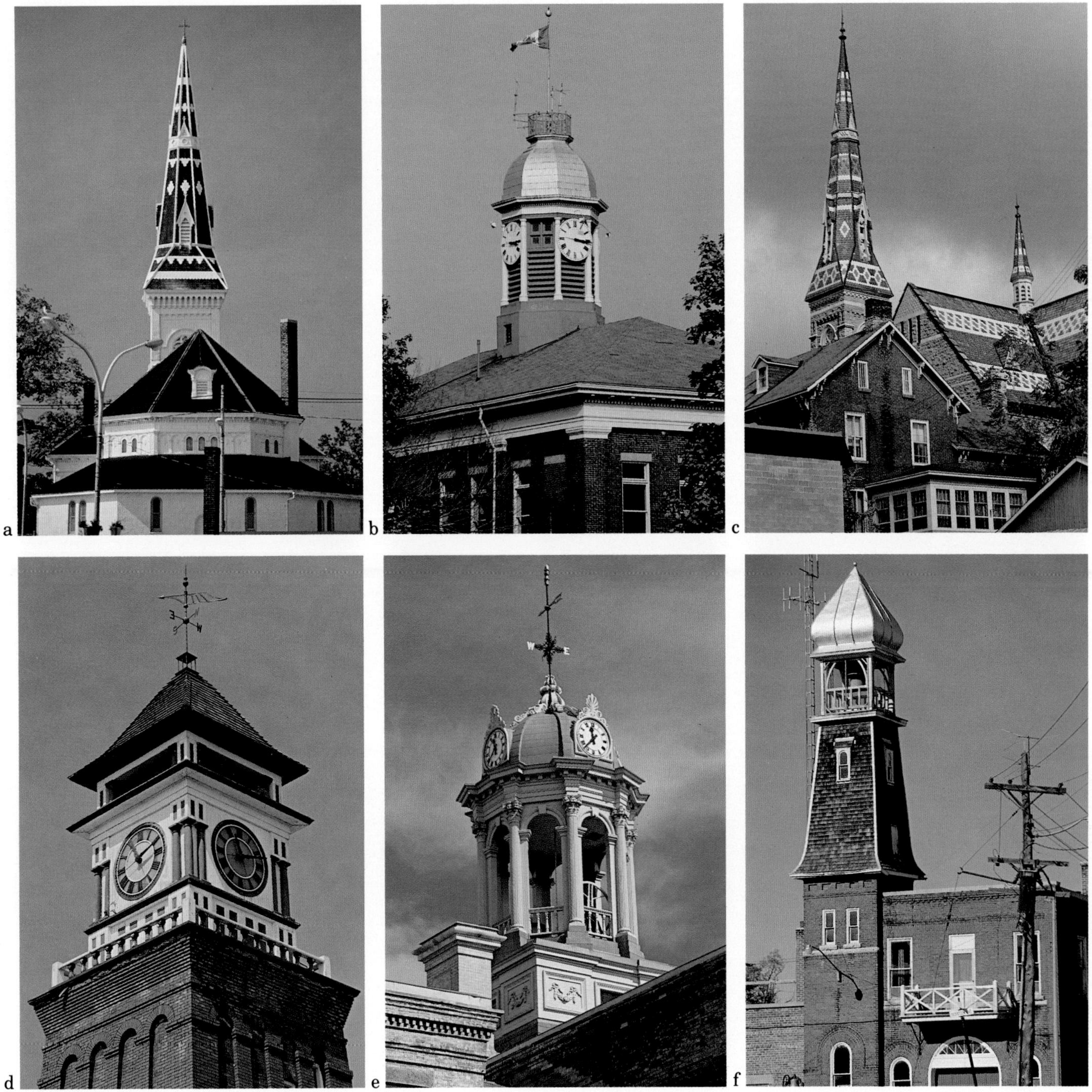
a
b
c
d
e
f

36 Cobourg
37 (a) Trenton
37 (b) Port Hope
37 (c) Brockville
37 (d) Gananoque
37 (e) Cobourg
37 (f) Campbellford

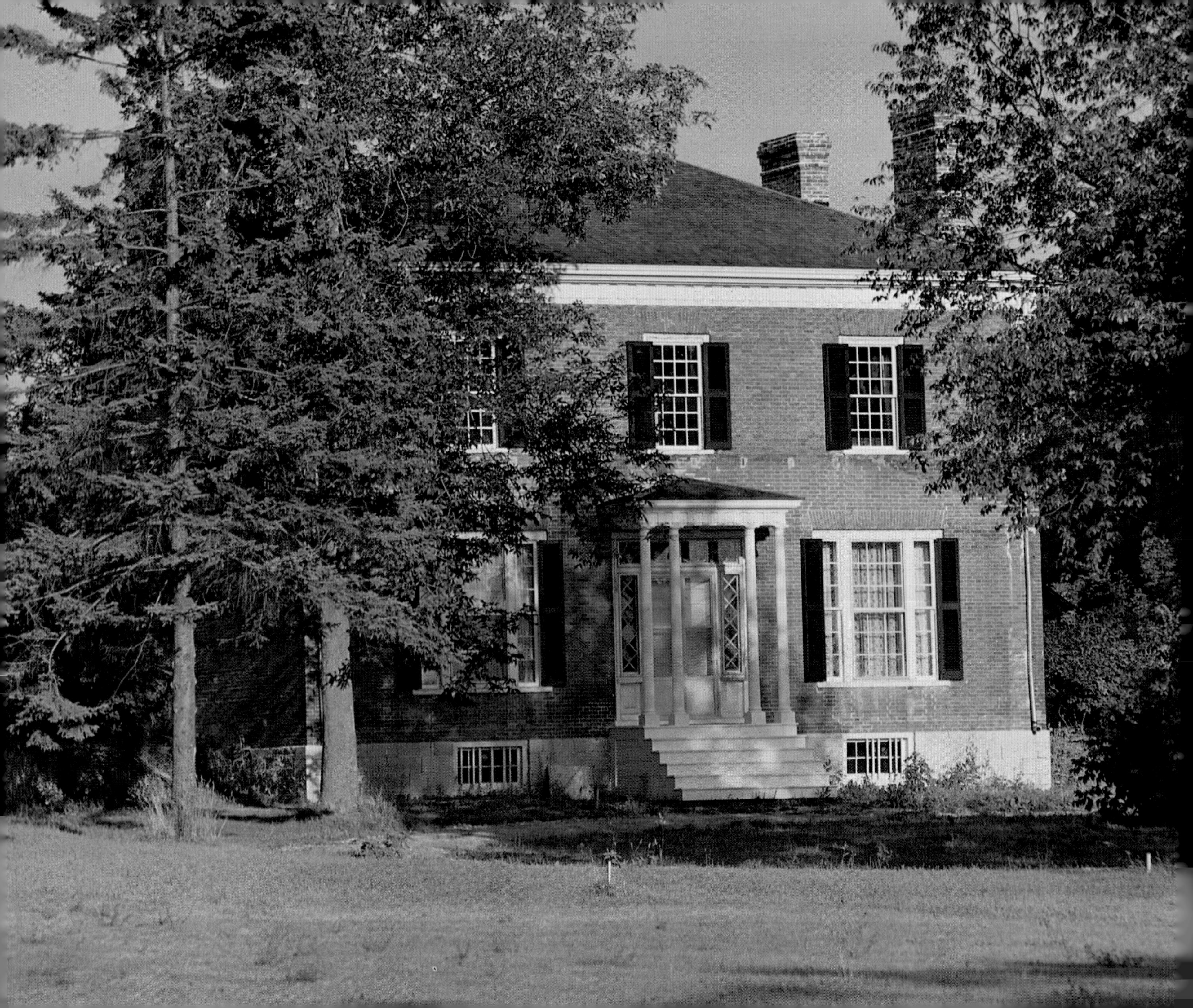

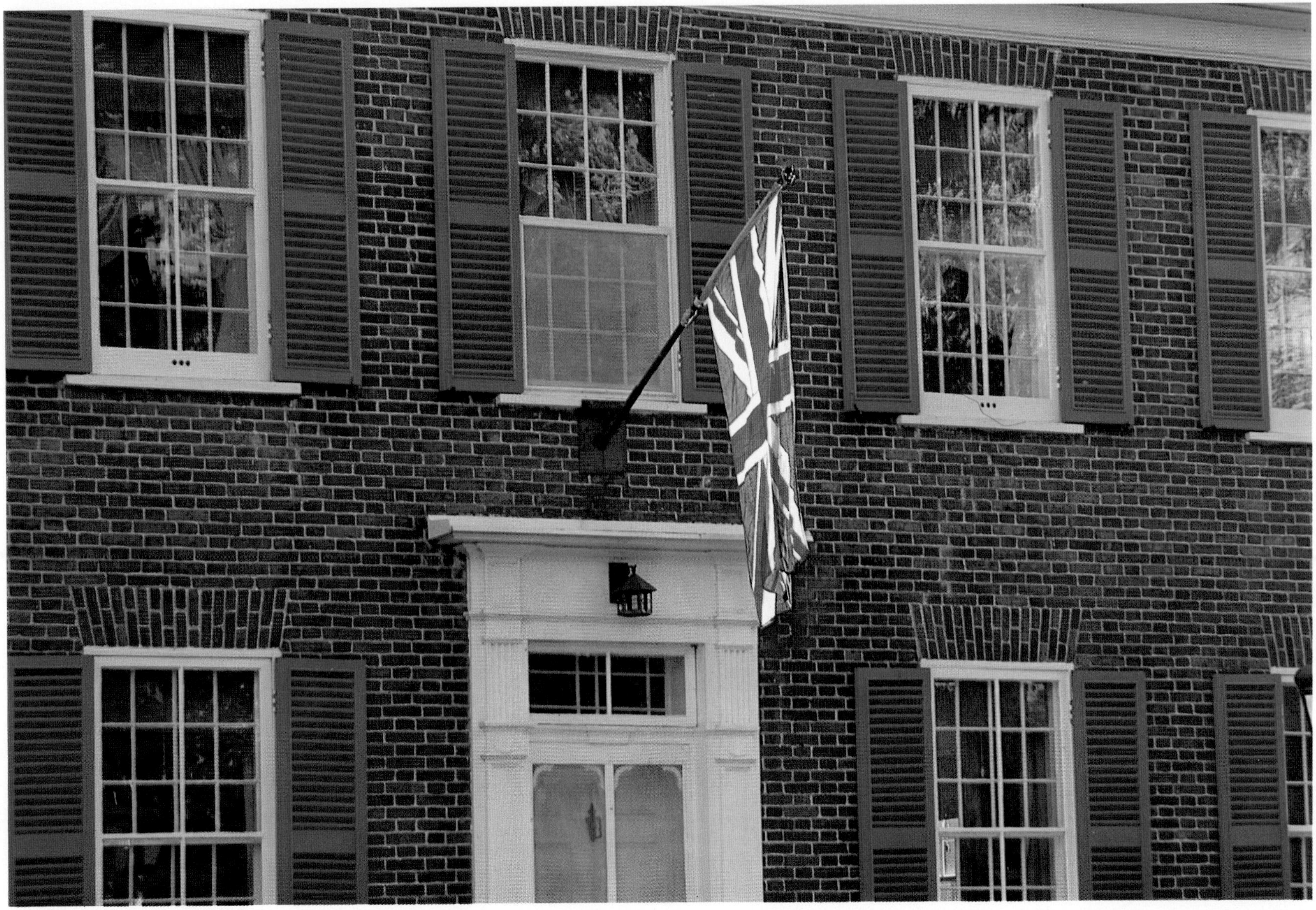

38 Macaulay House, Picton
39 Spalding House, Grafton

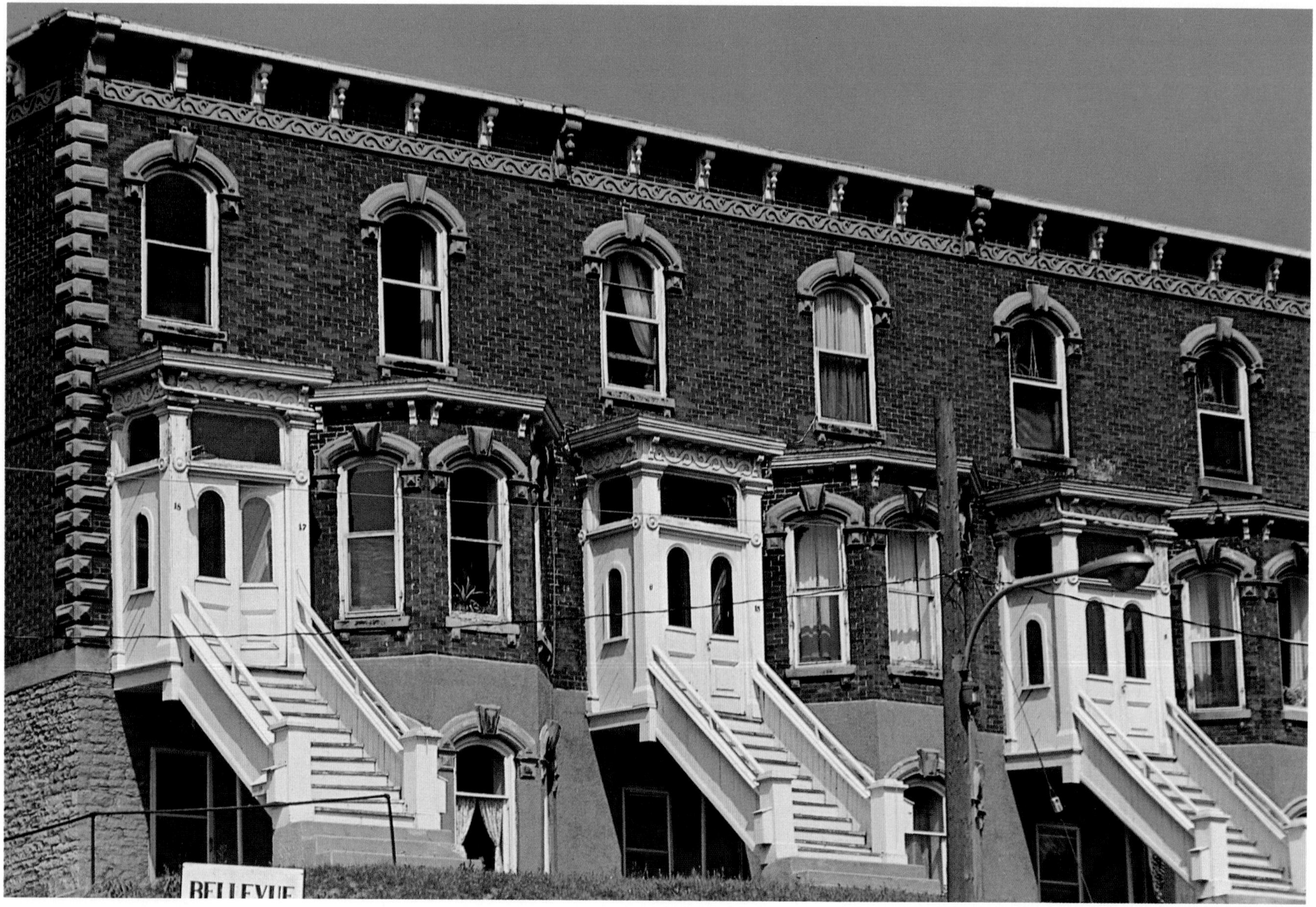
BELLEVUE

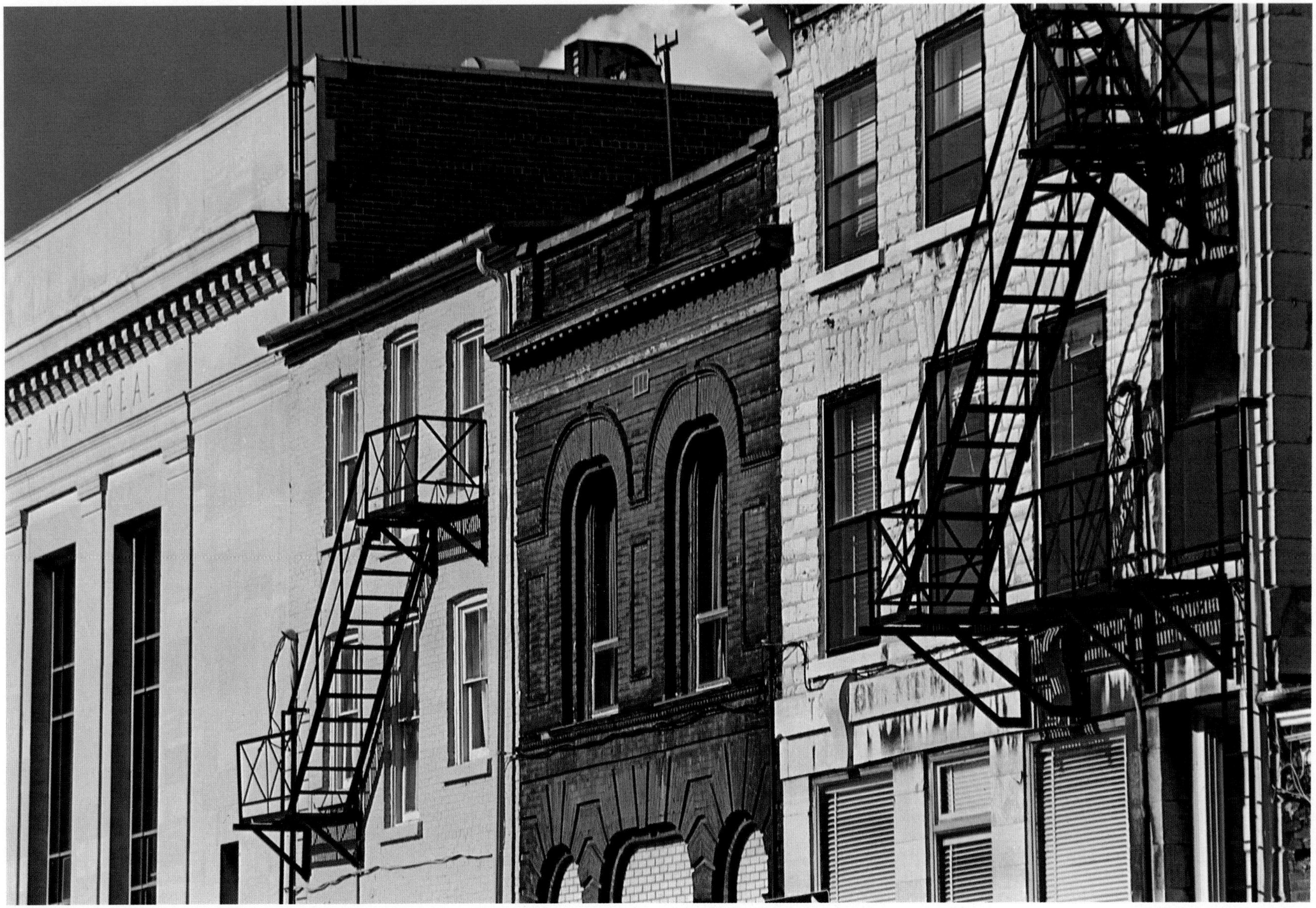
OF MONTREAL

41 Kingston

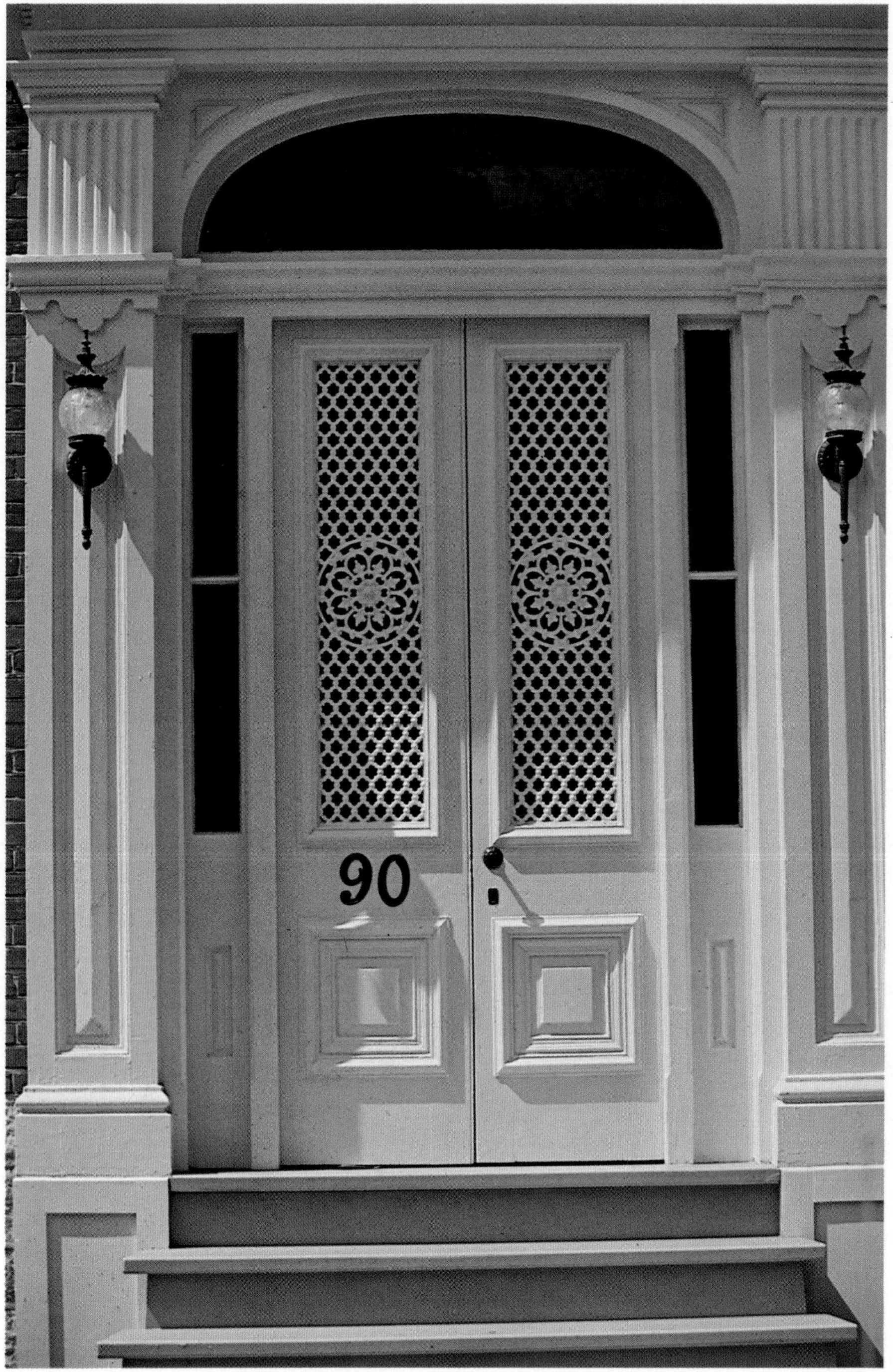
90

42 Gananoque
43 Prescott

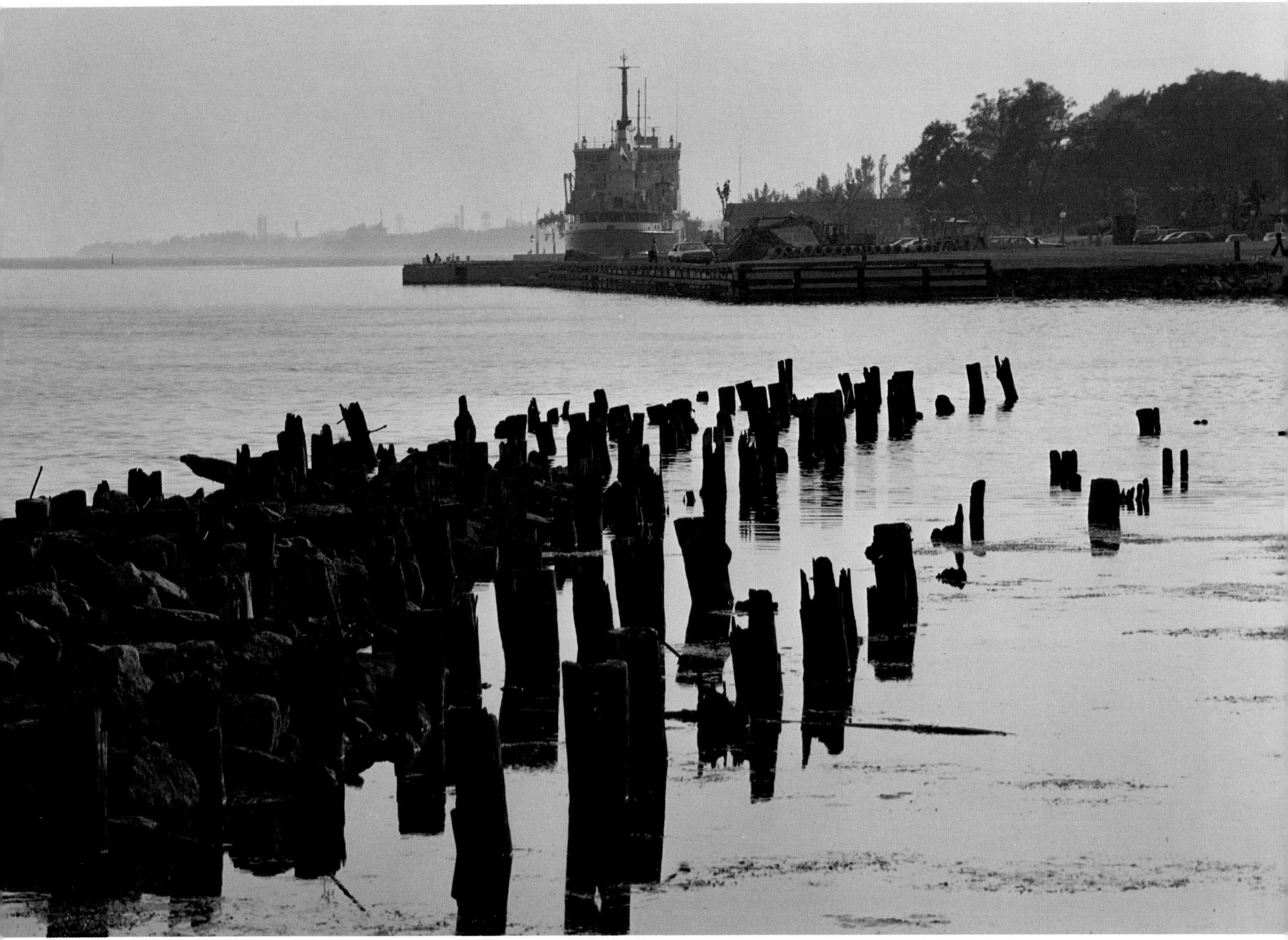

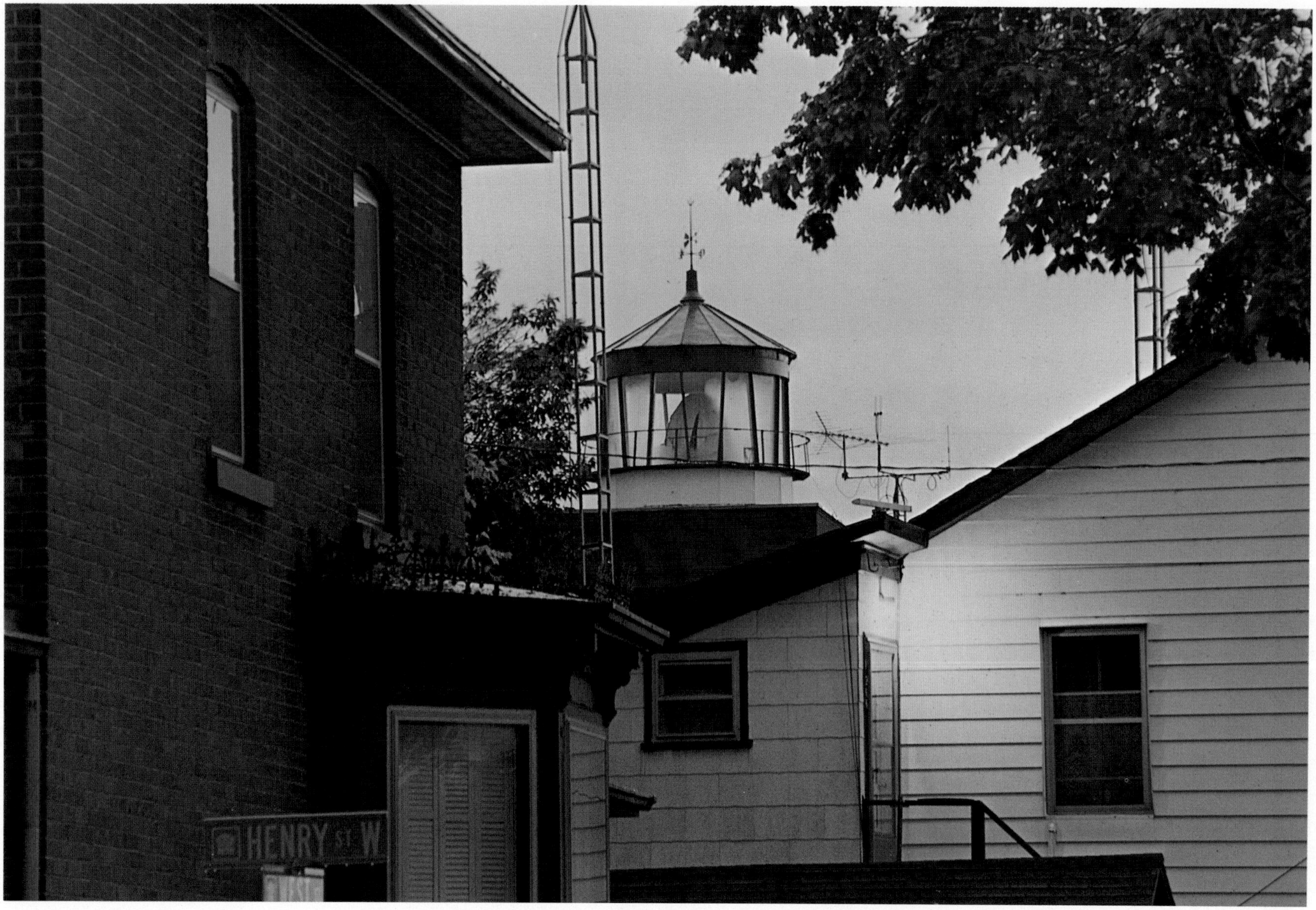
HENRY ST W

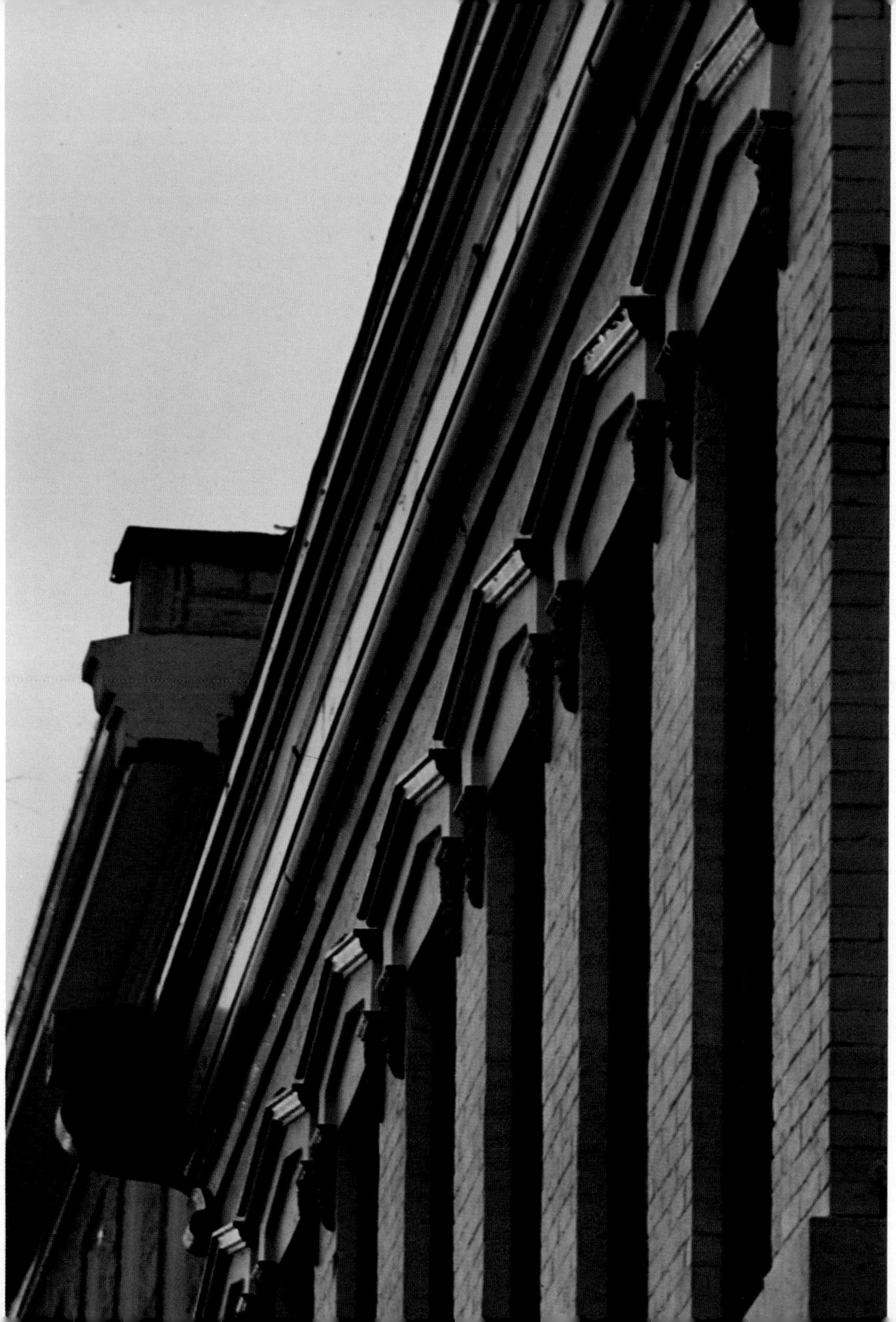

45 Kingston

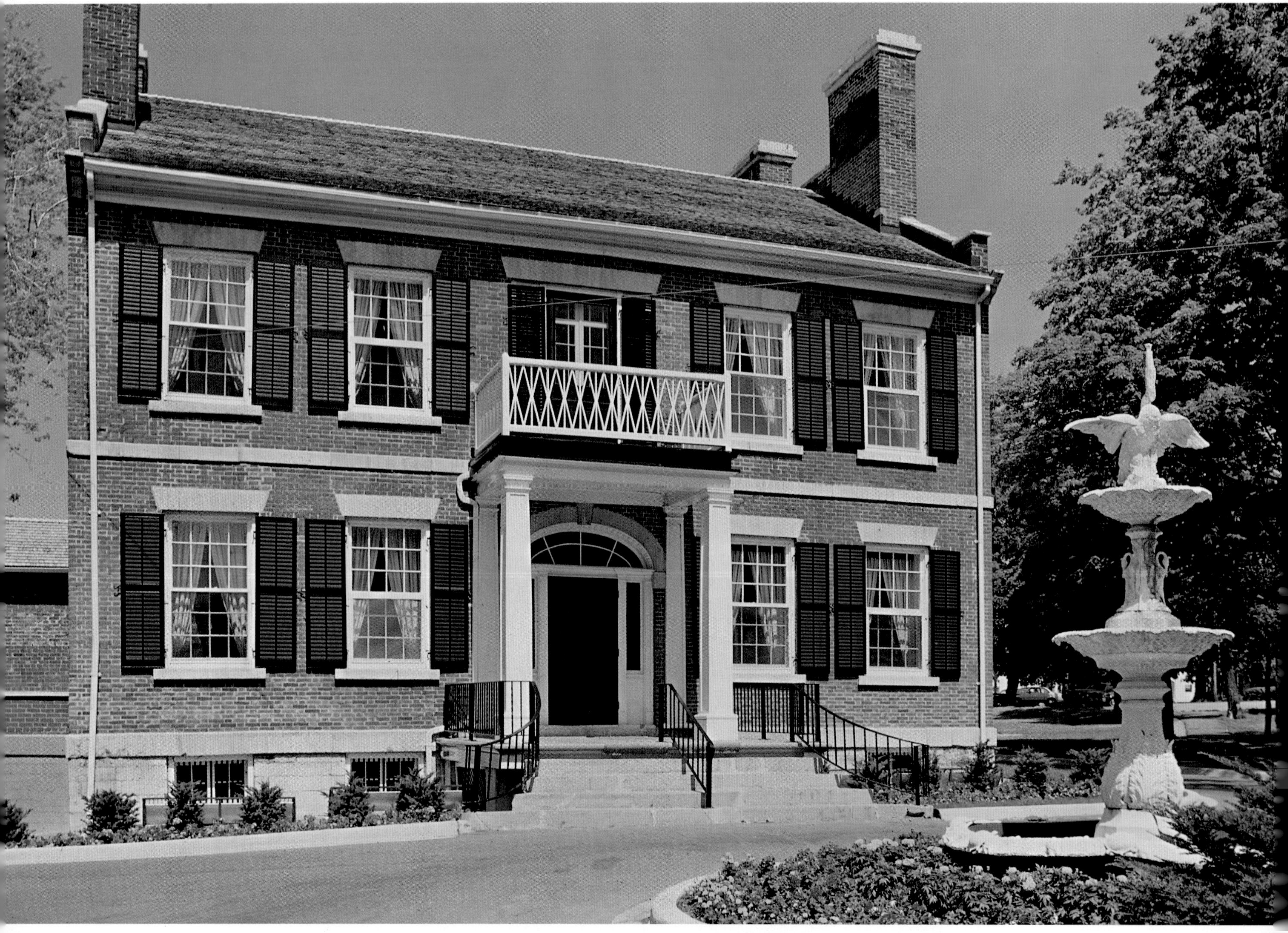

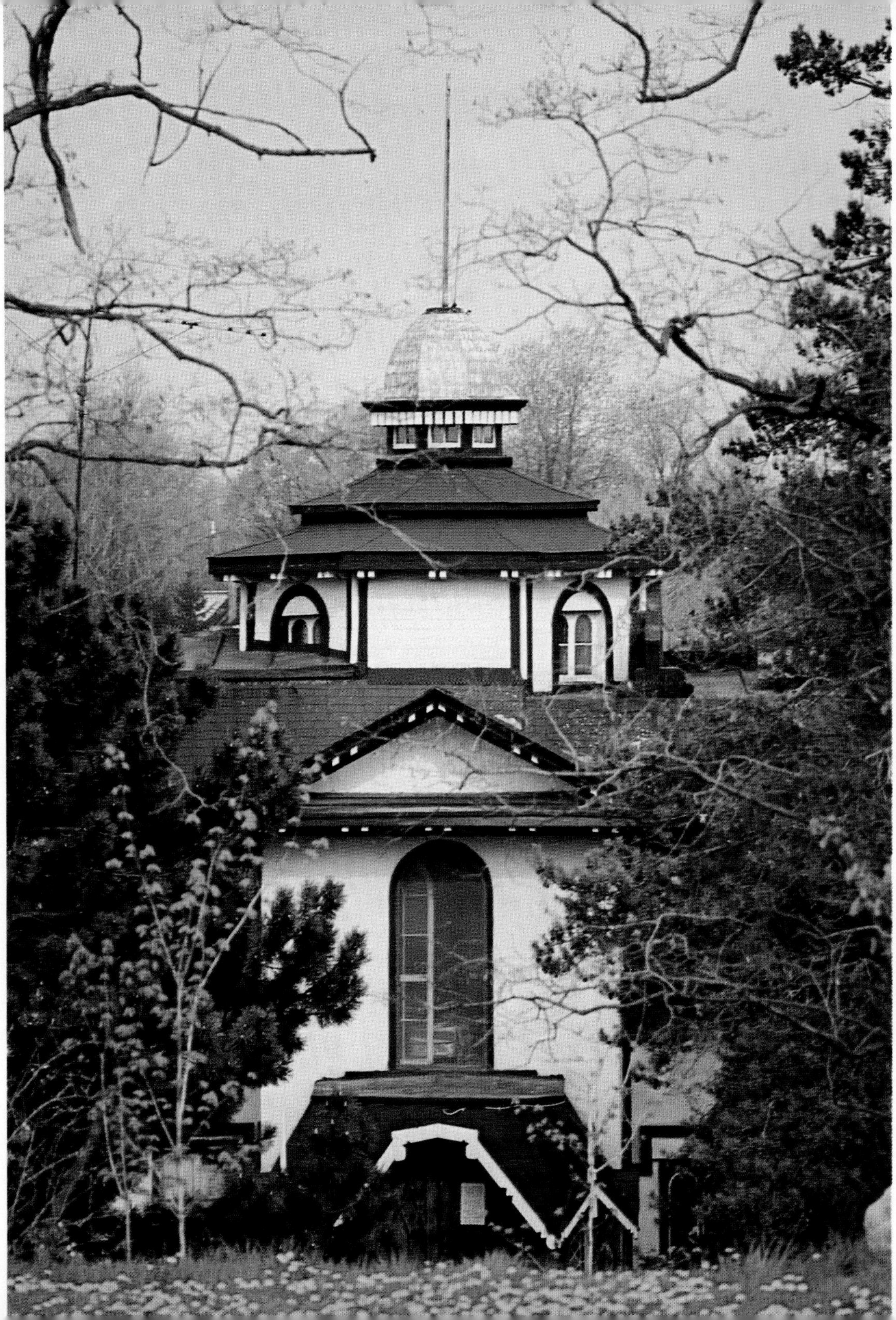

46 McDonald House, Gananoque
47 Picton

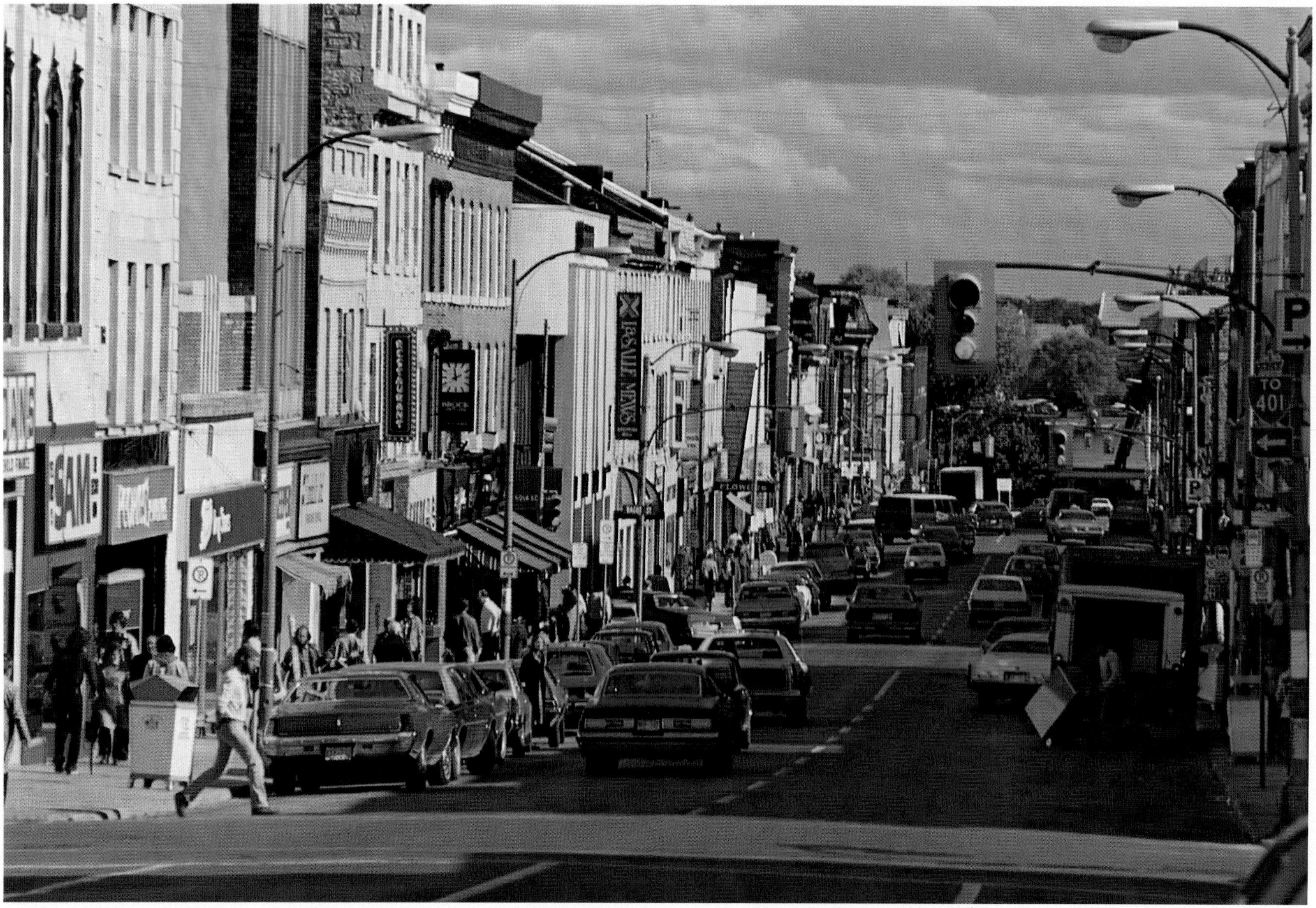
RESTAURANT
BROCK
LaSALLE MEWS
P
TO
401

48 Kingston
49 Courthouse, Brockville

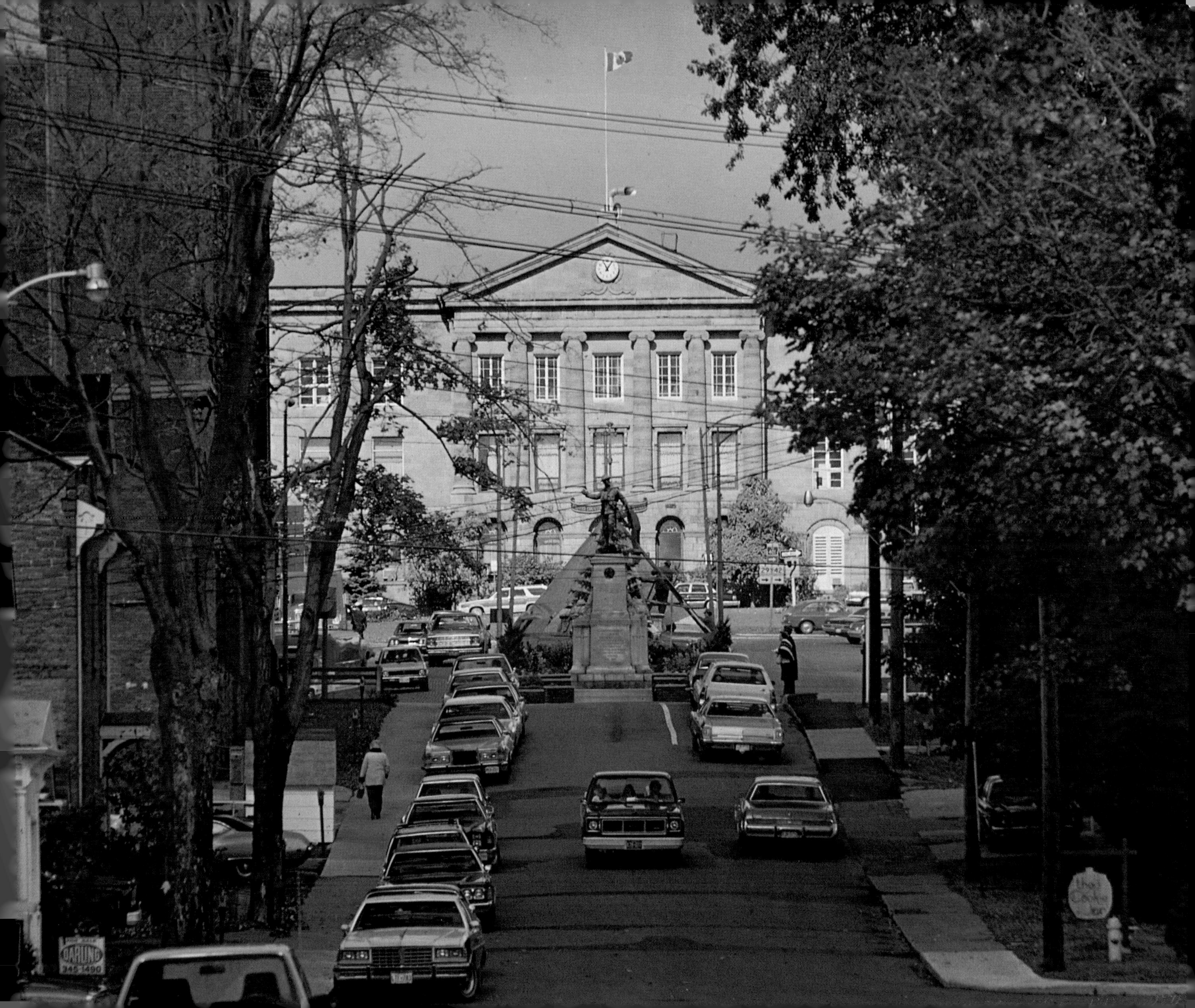

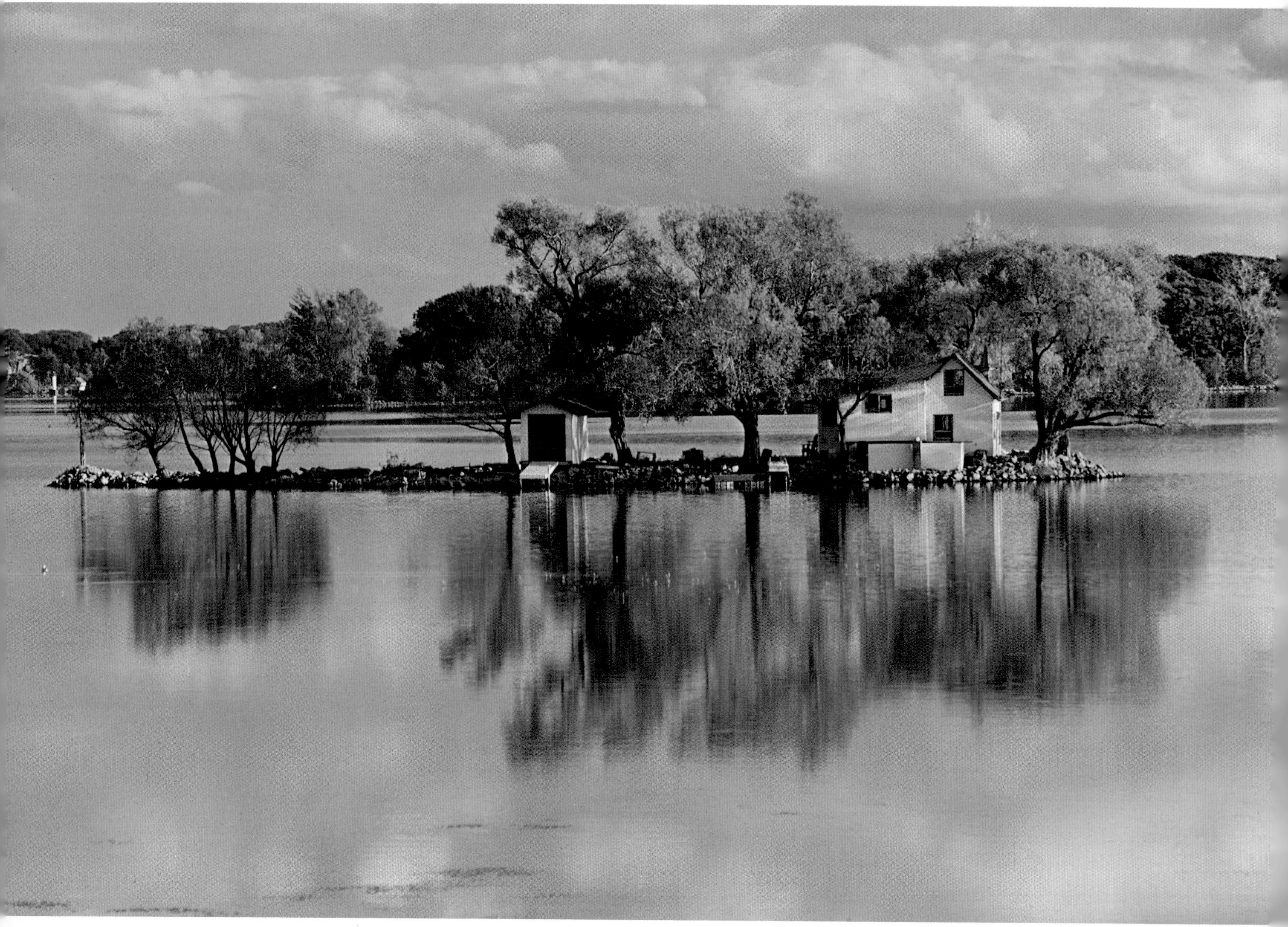

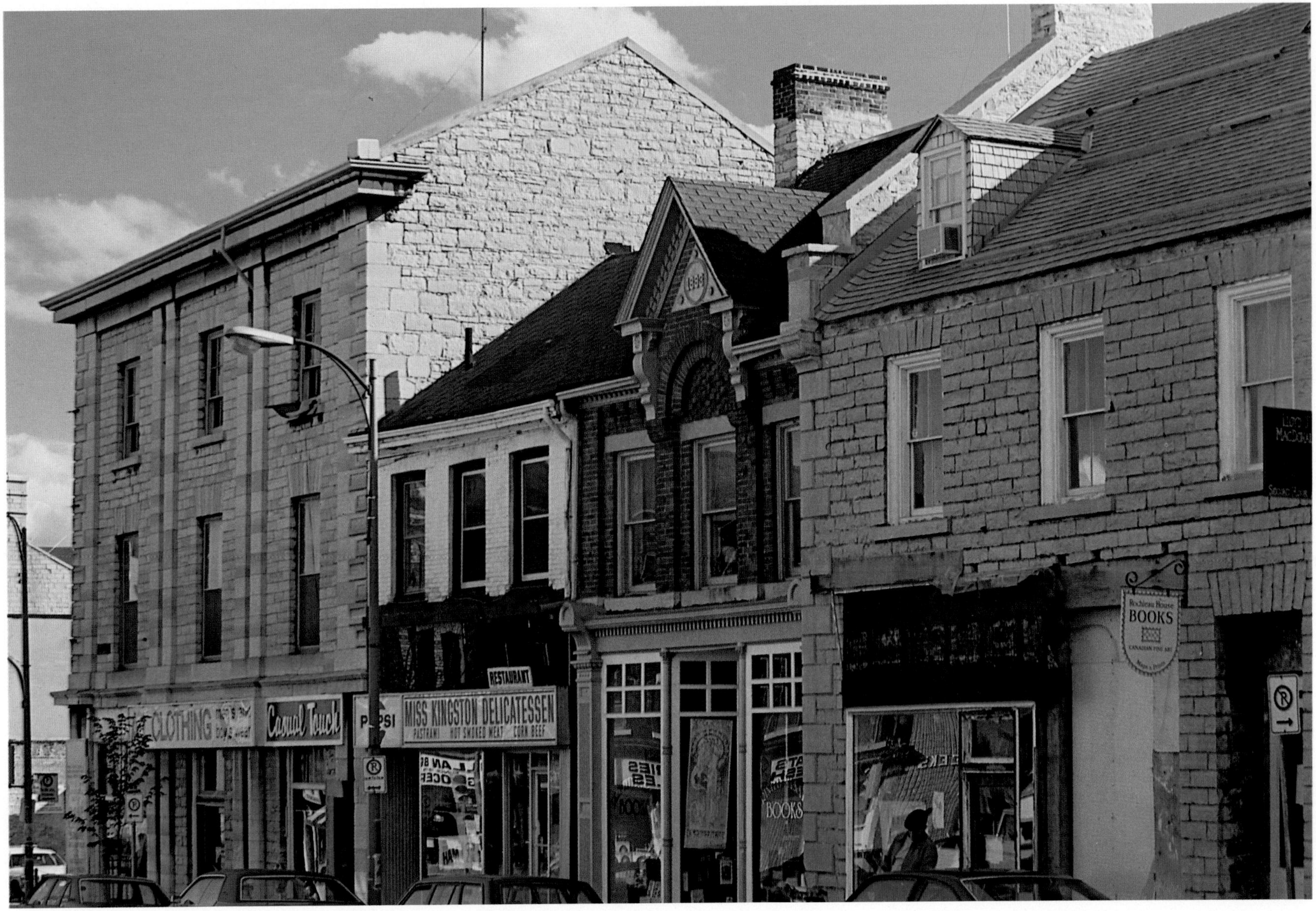
RESTAURANT
CLOTHING
Casual Touch
MISS KINGSTON DELICATESSEN
PASTRAMI HOT SMOKED MEAT CORN BEEF
BOOKS
CANADIAN FINE ART
BOOKS

50 St Lawrence Islands, near Gananoque
51 Kingston

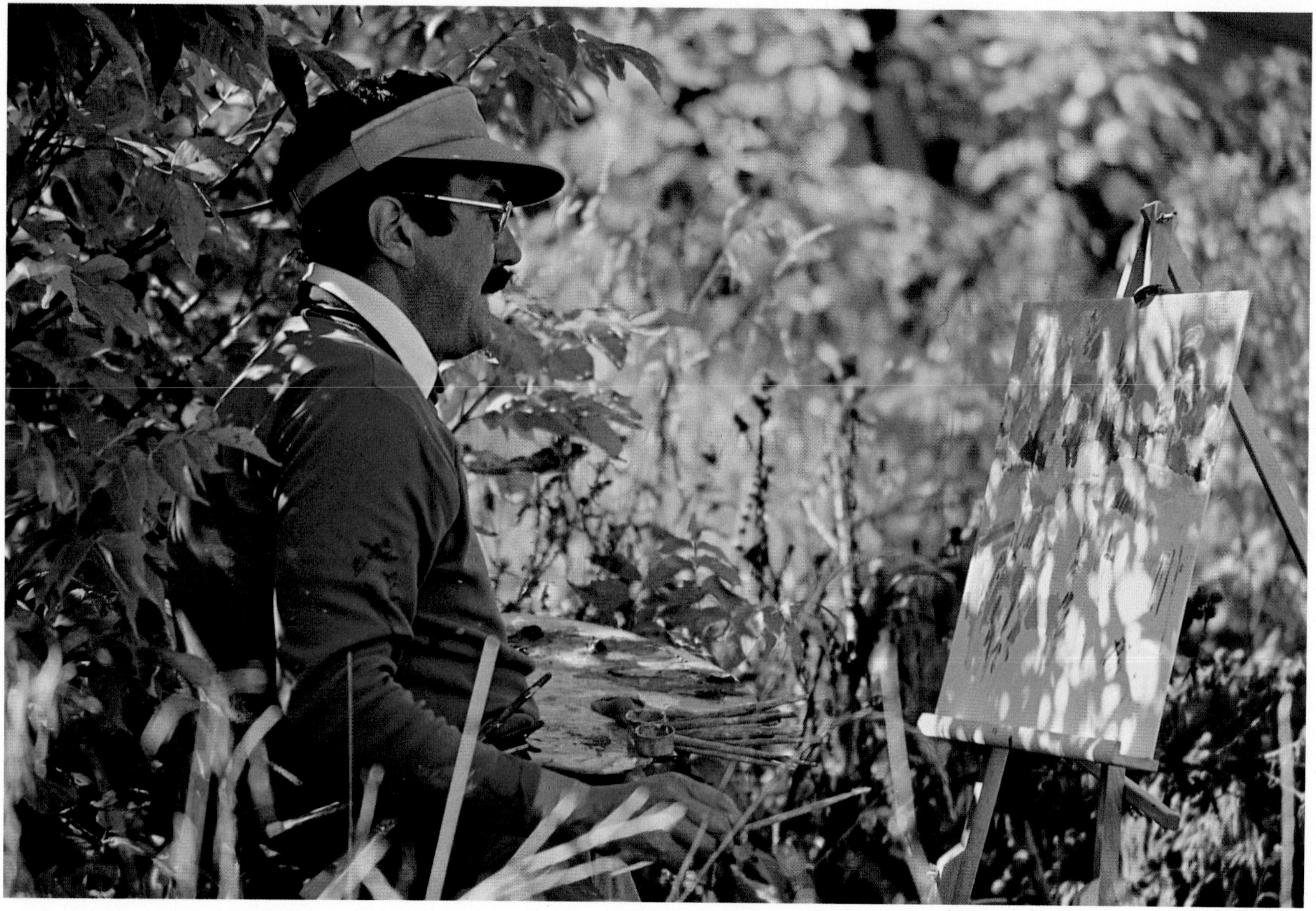

52 Campbellford
53 Vernonville

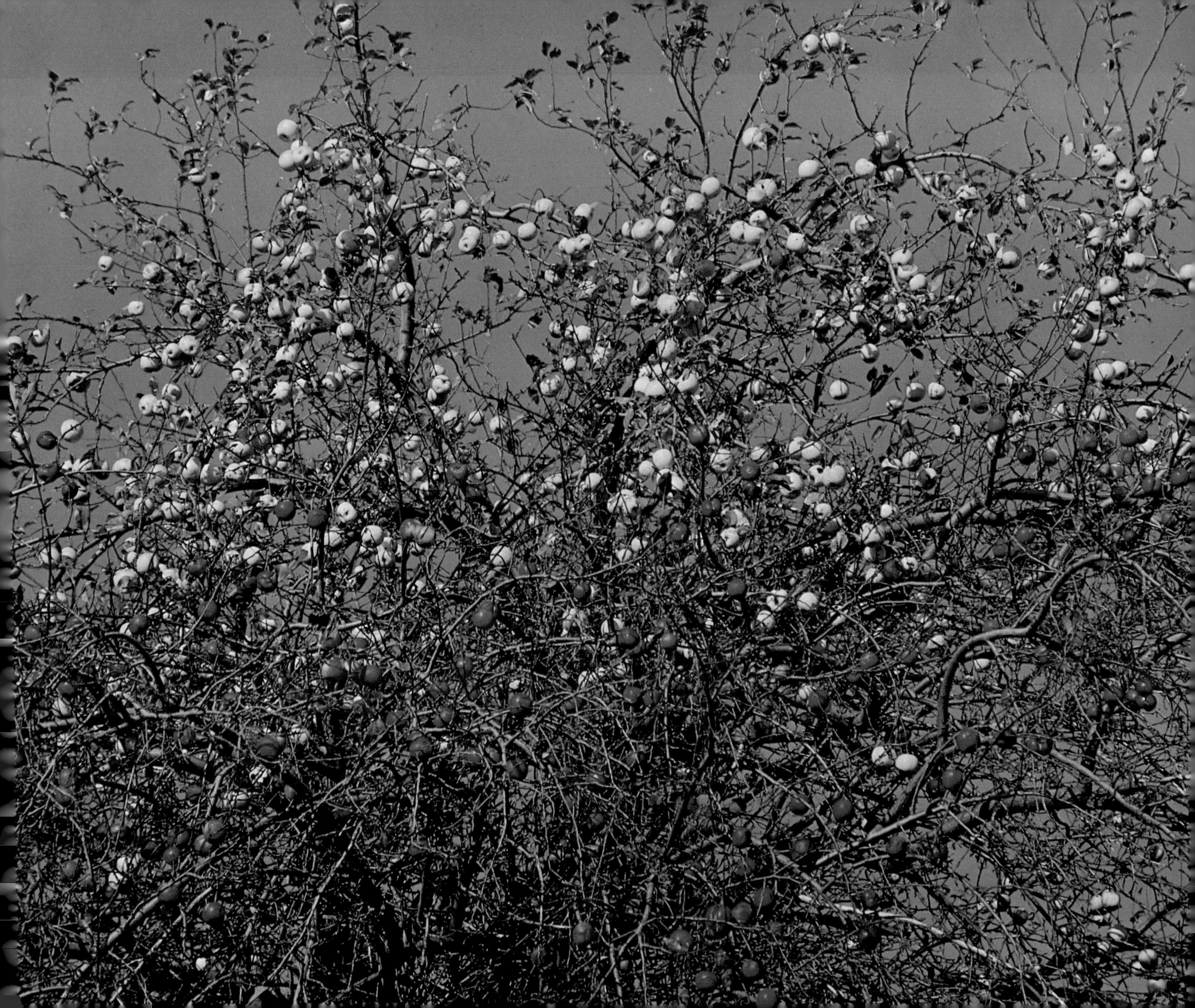

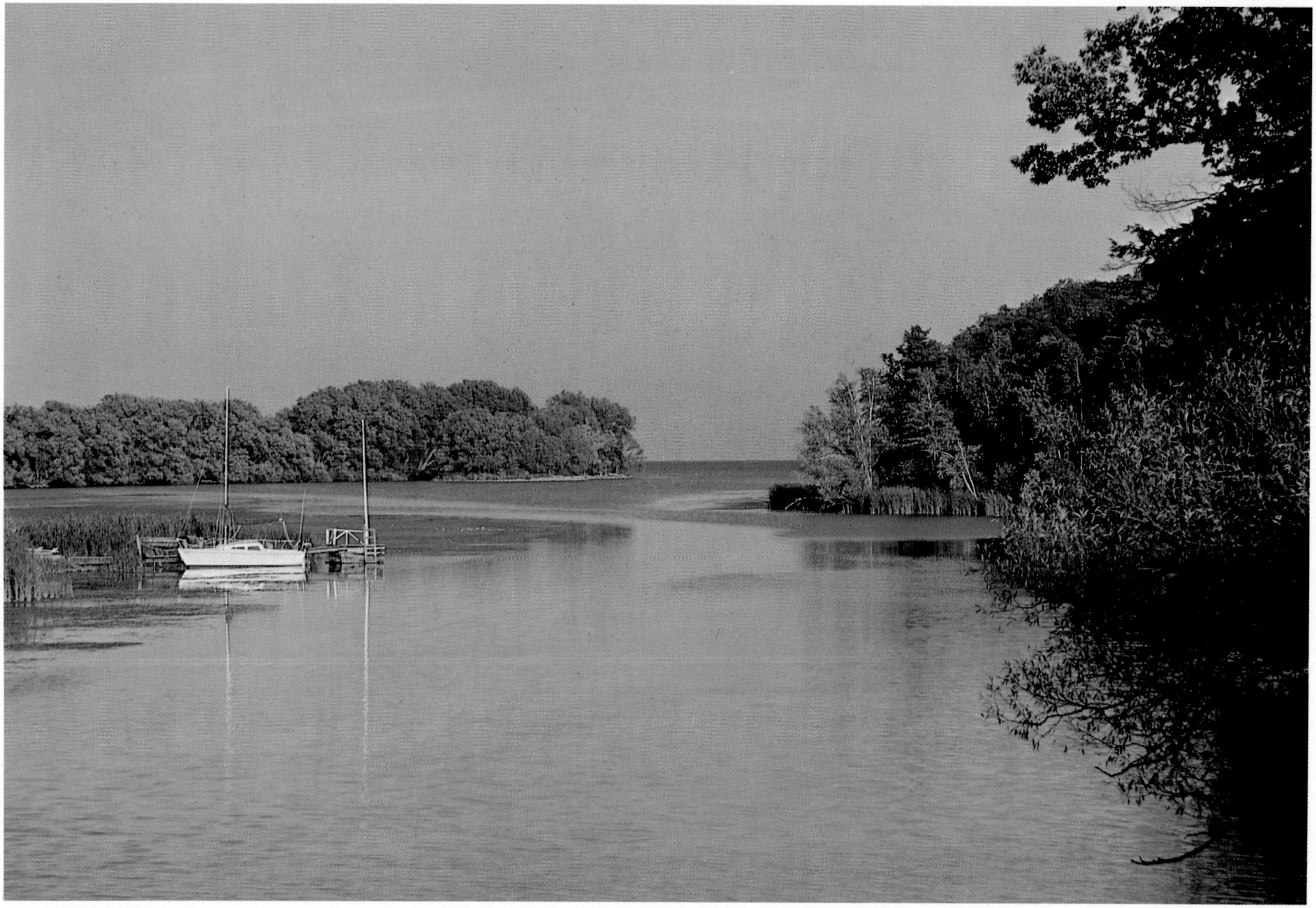

54 Black River
55 Near Bloomfield

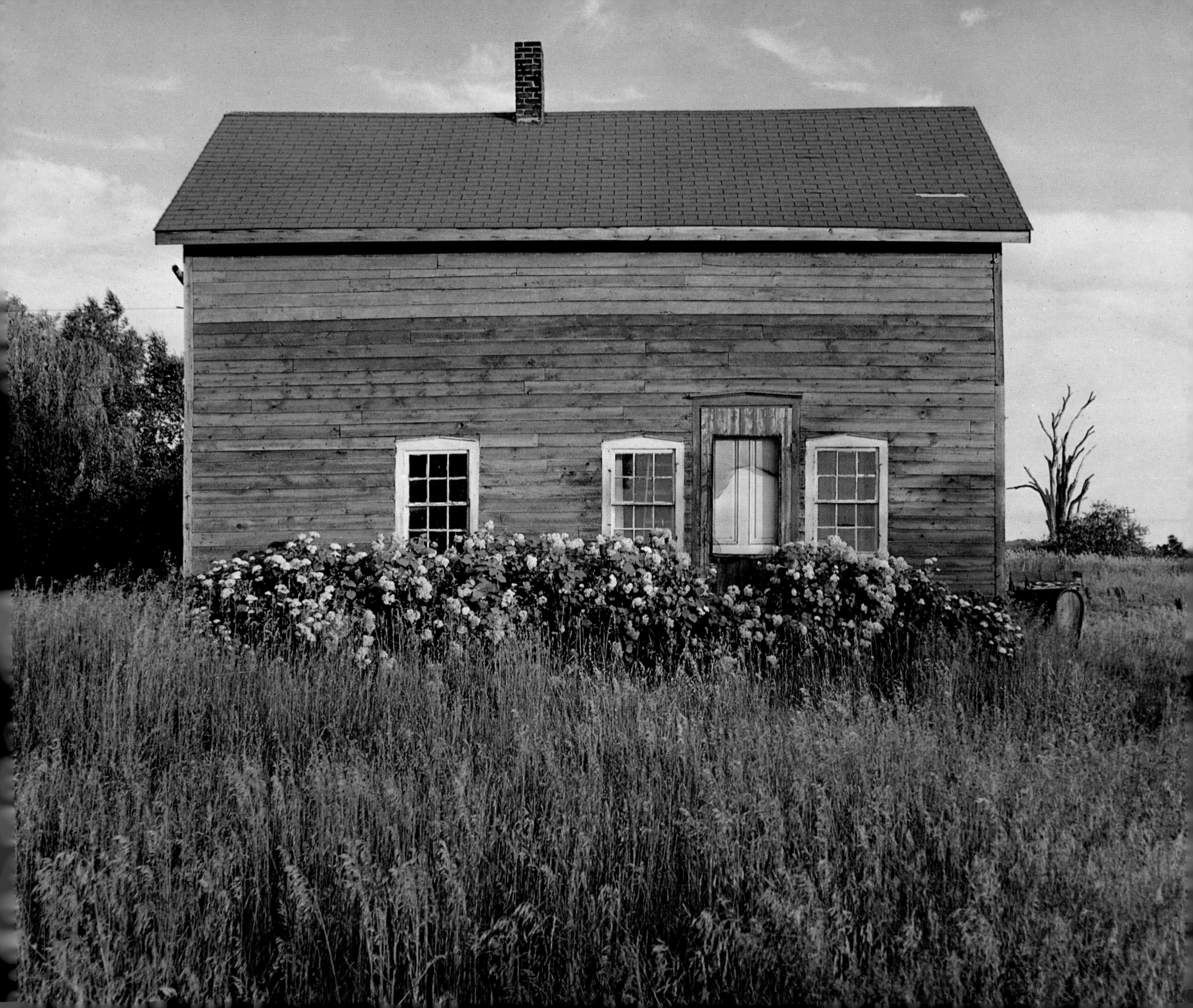

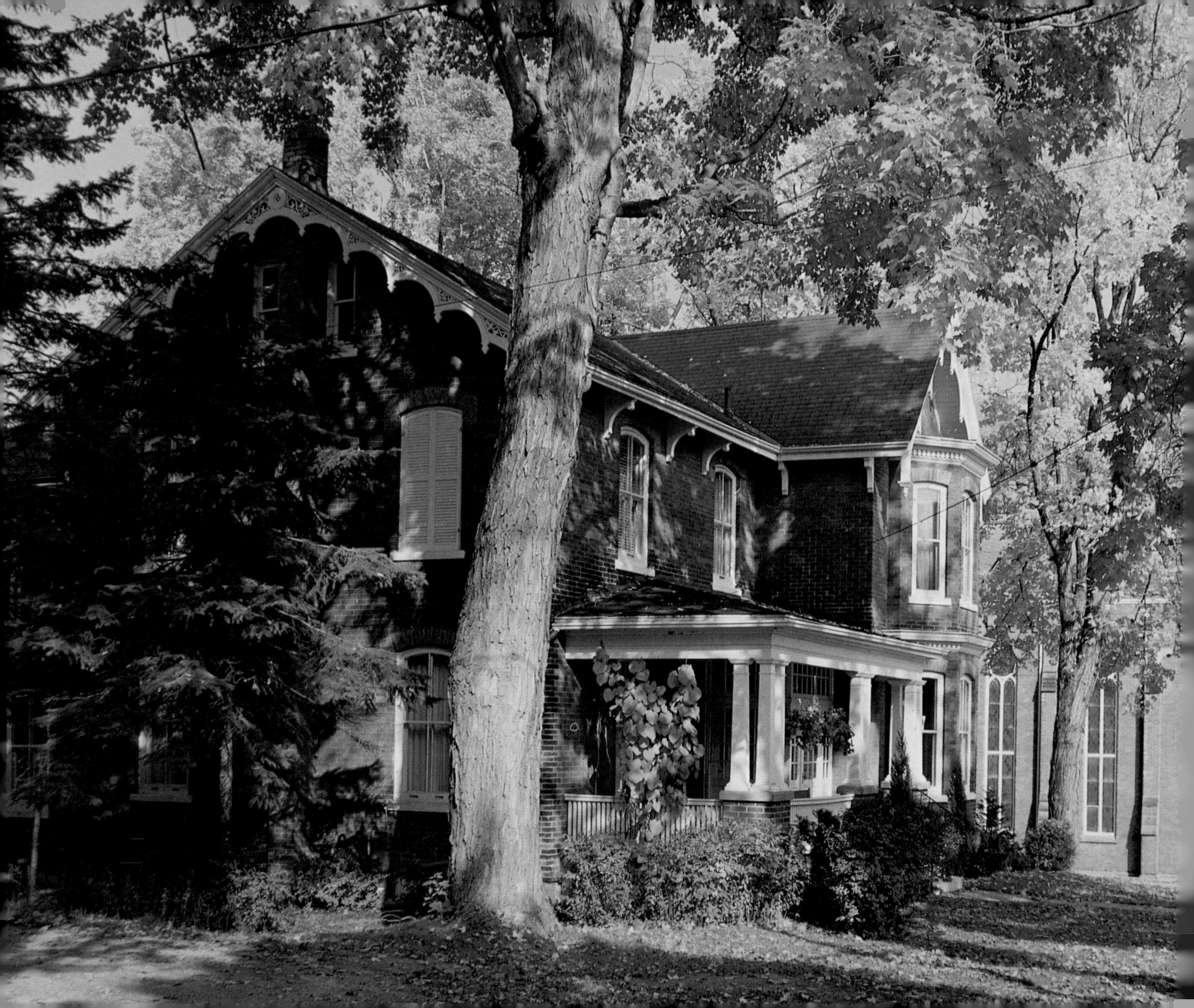

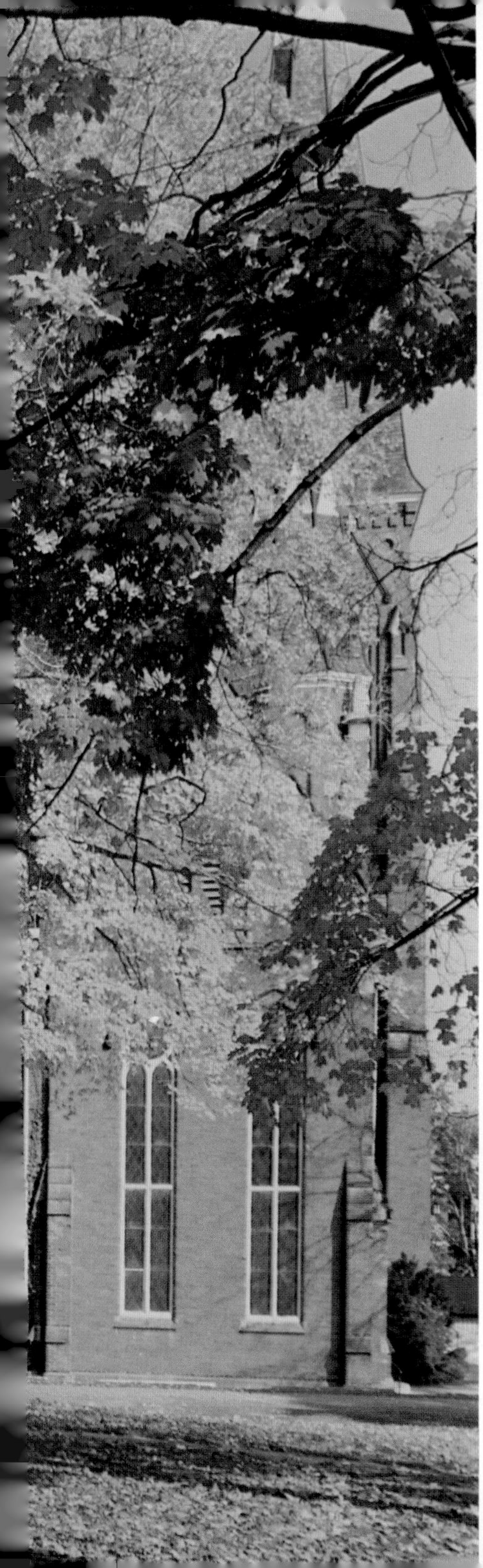

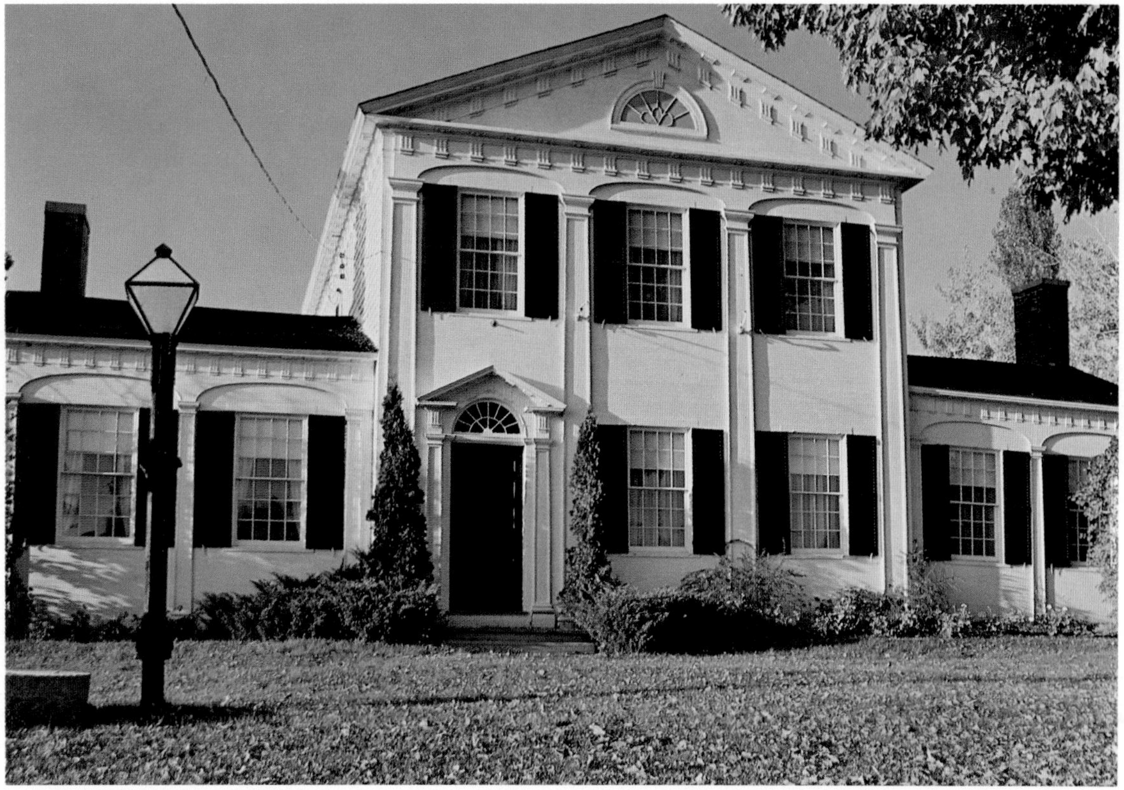

56 Port Hope
57 'The Poplars', the Barnum House, Grafton

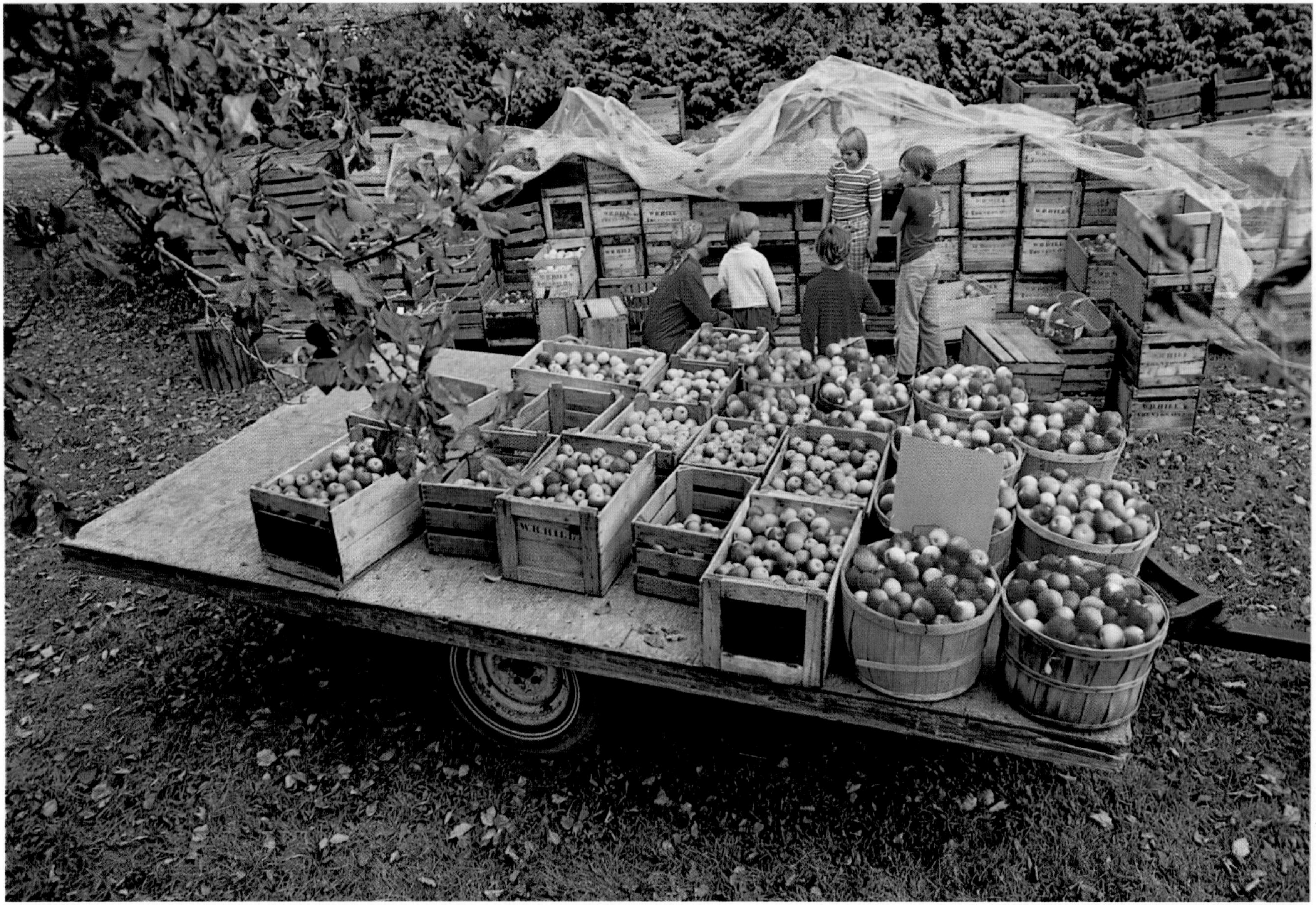
W.R.HILL

58 Near Carrying Place
59 Near Ameliasburg

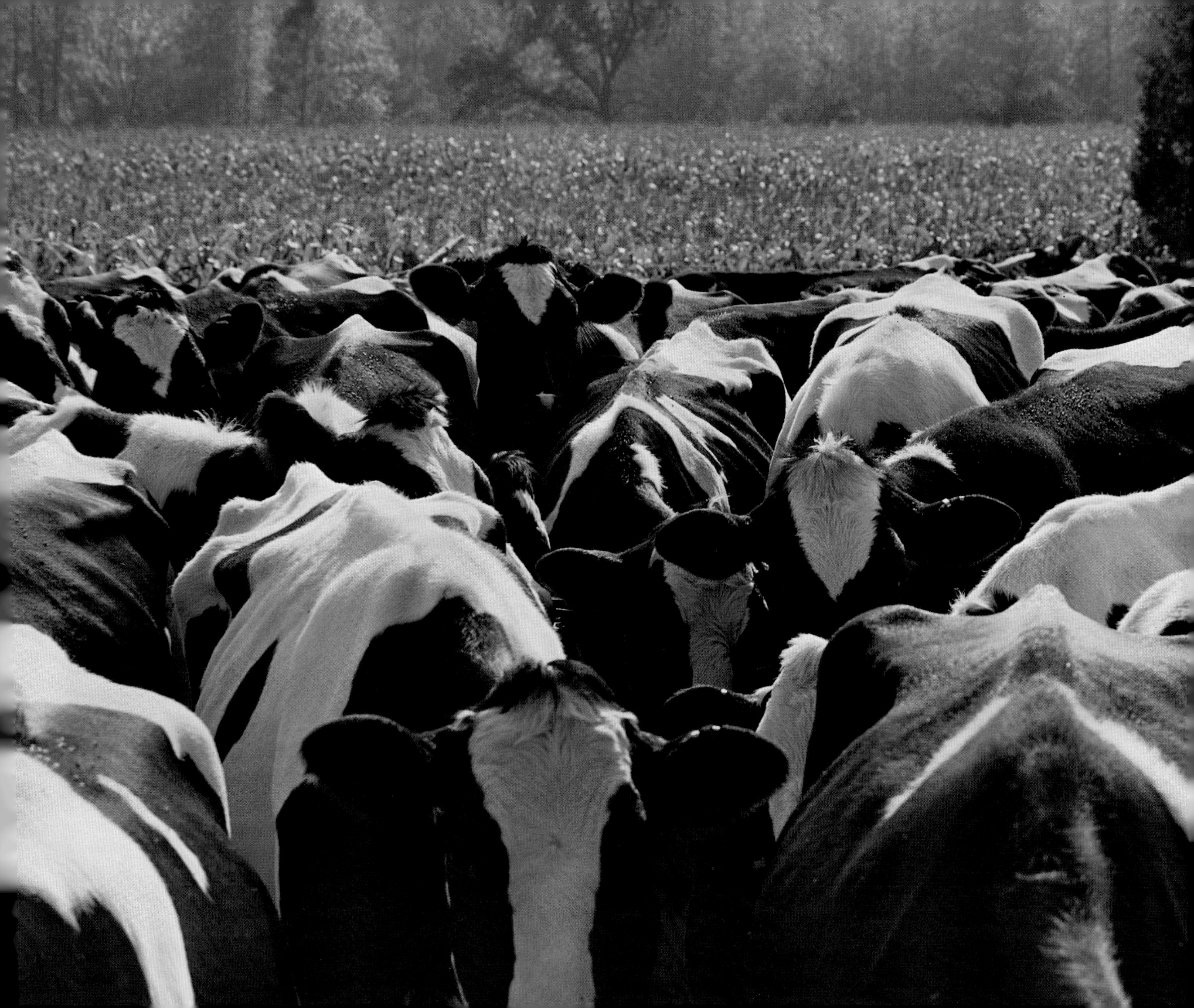

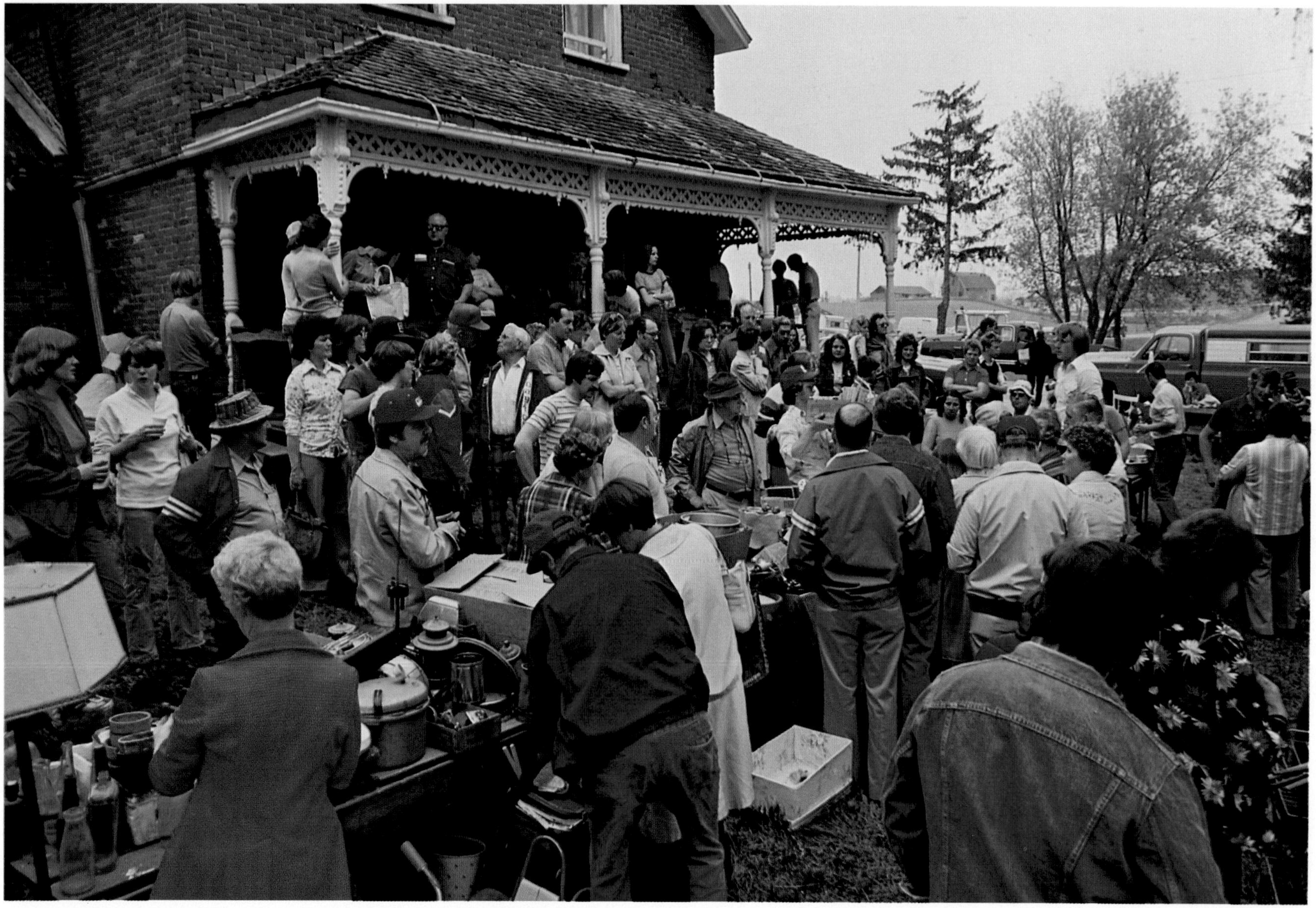

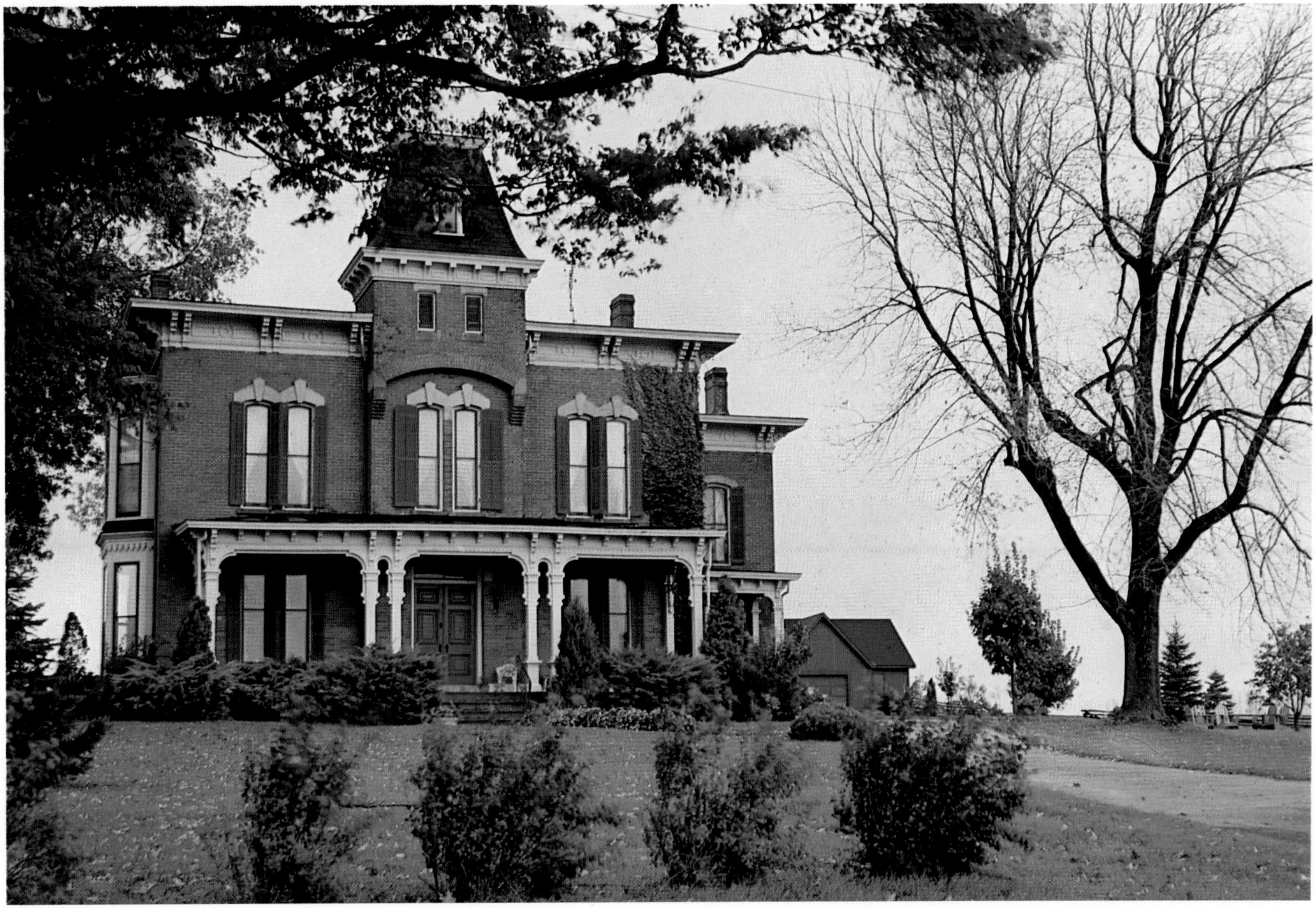

61 Near Prescott

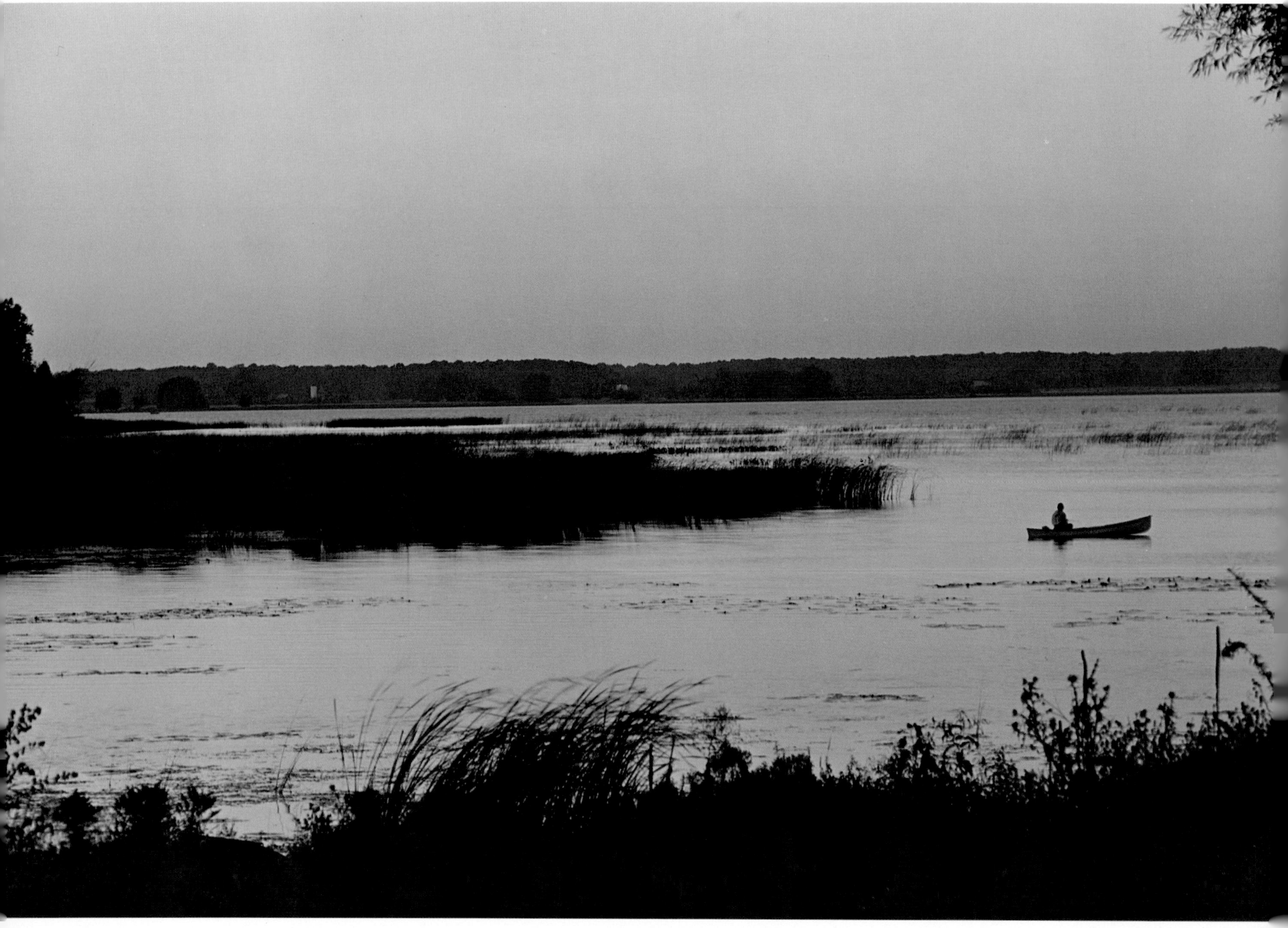

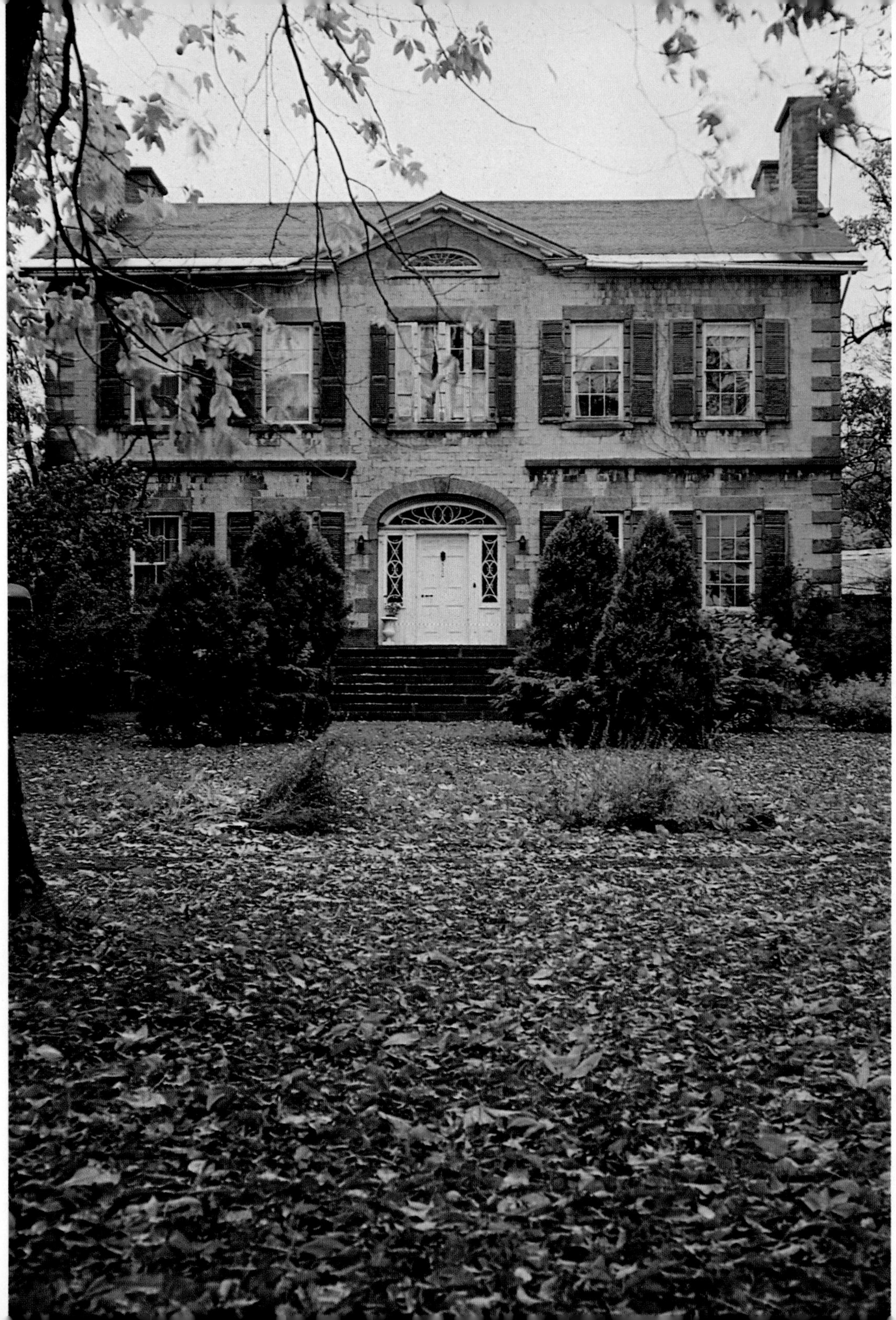

62 Near Salmon Point
63 Alphaeus Jones House, Prescott

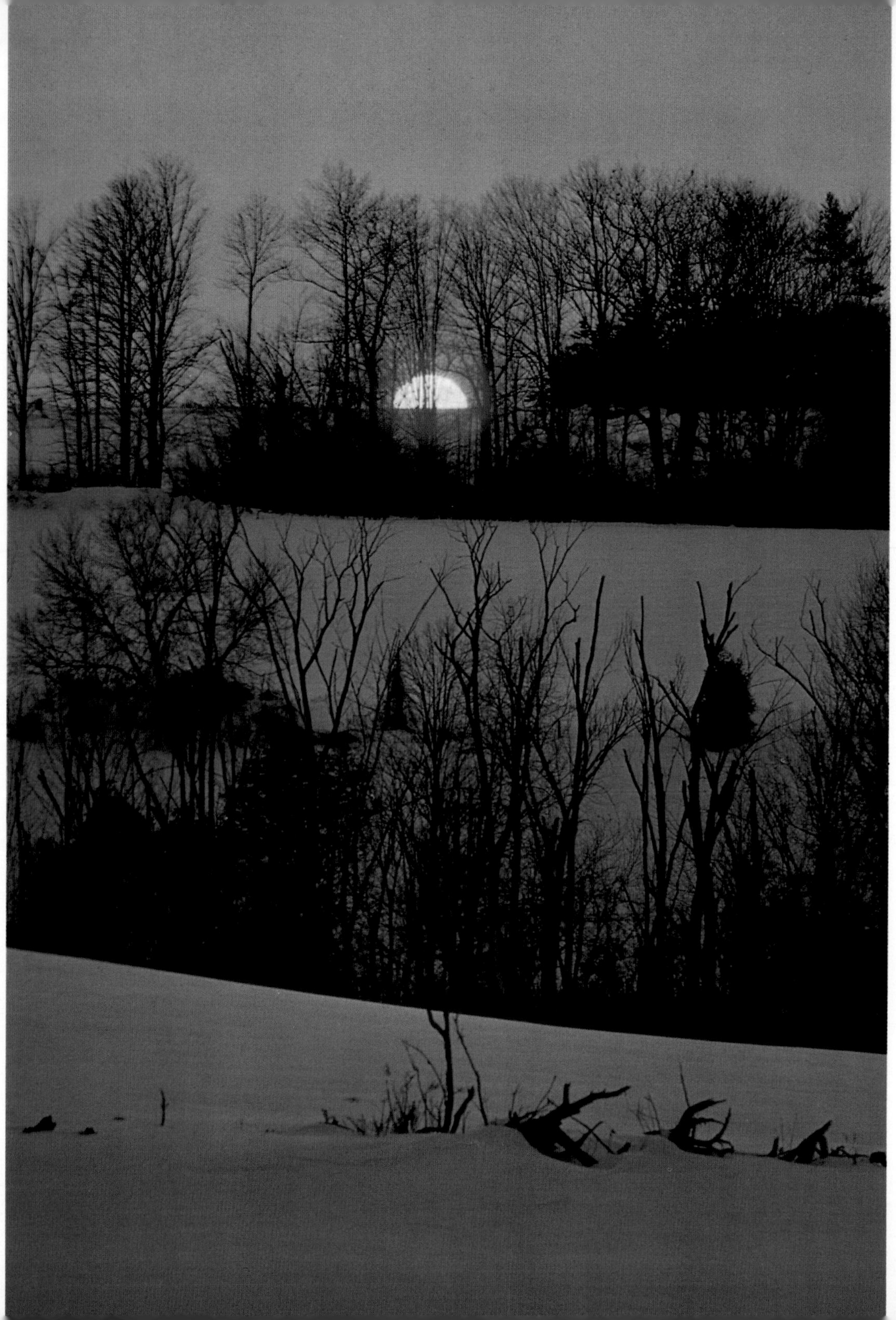

64 Near Godolphin Road

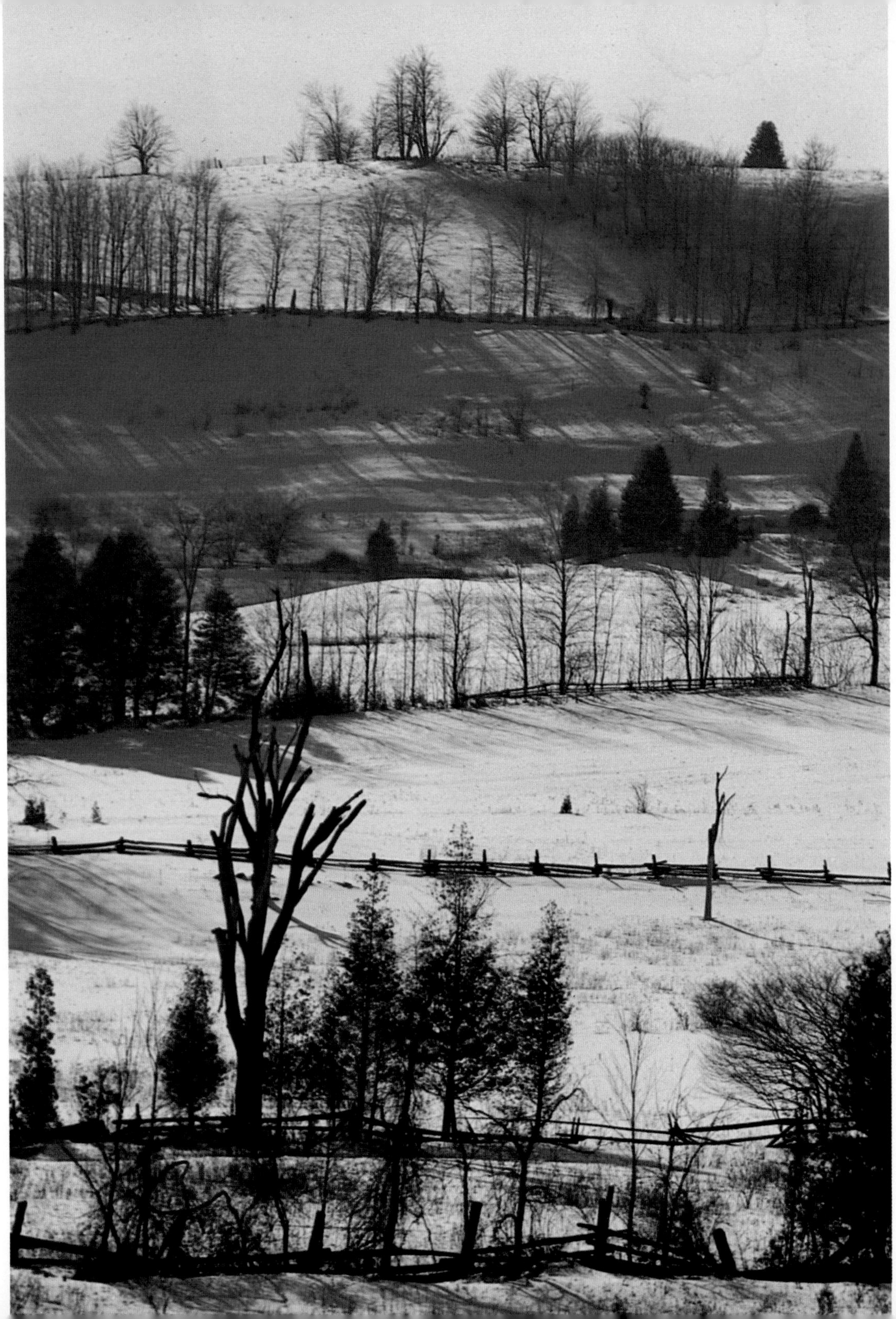

65 Near Godolphin Road

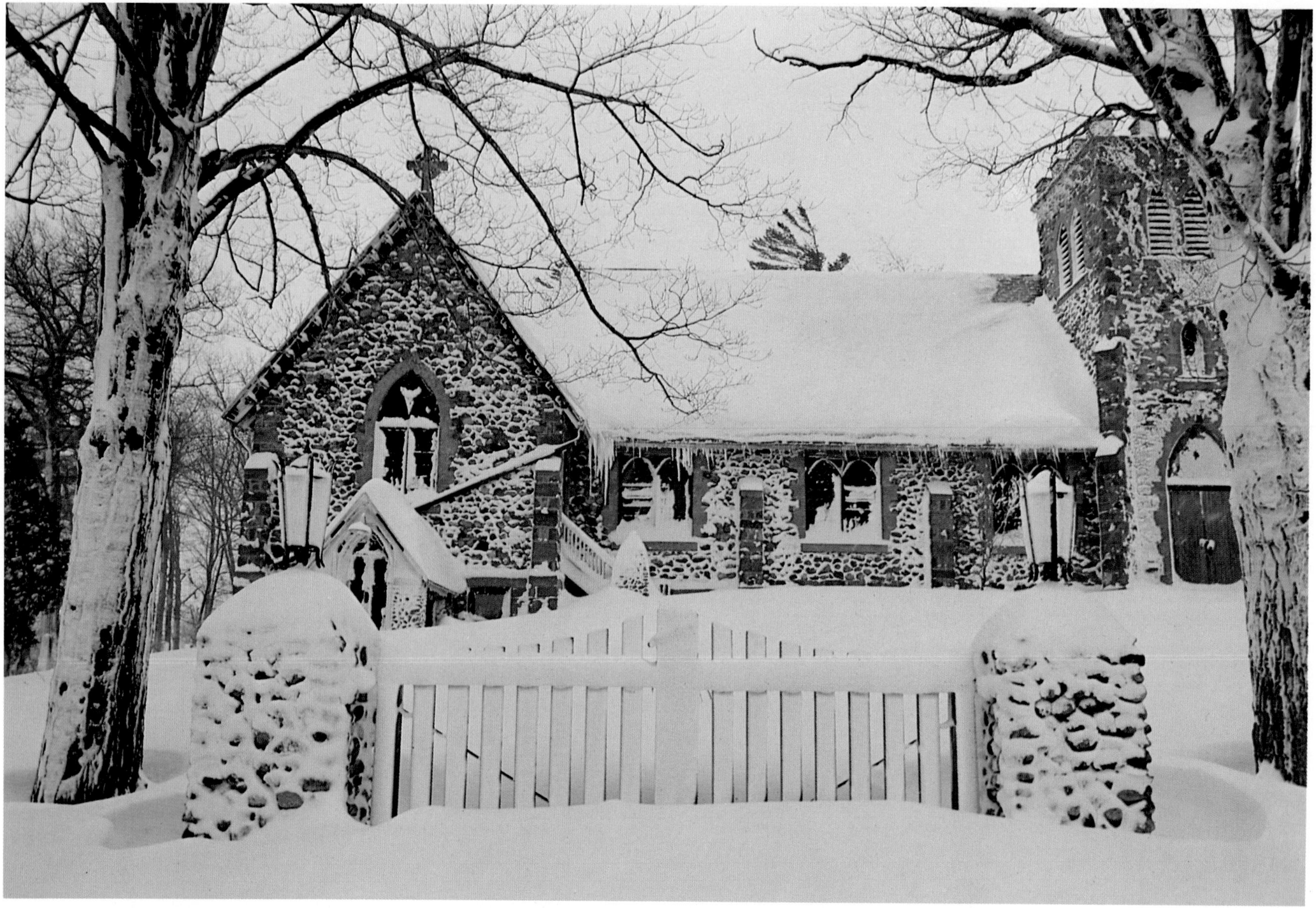

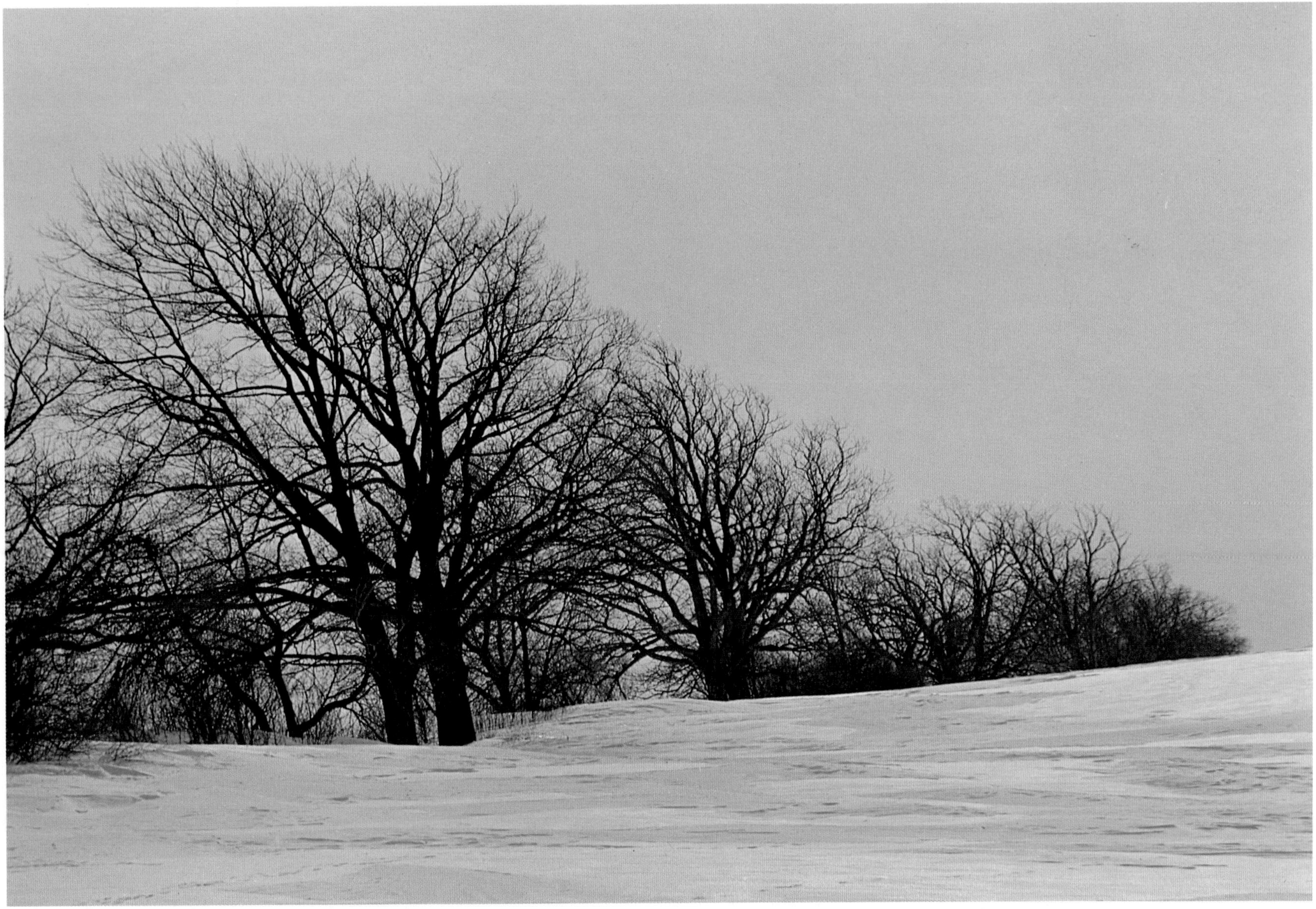

67 Near Harwood

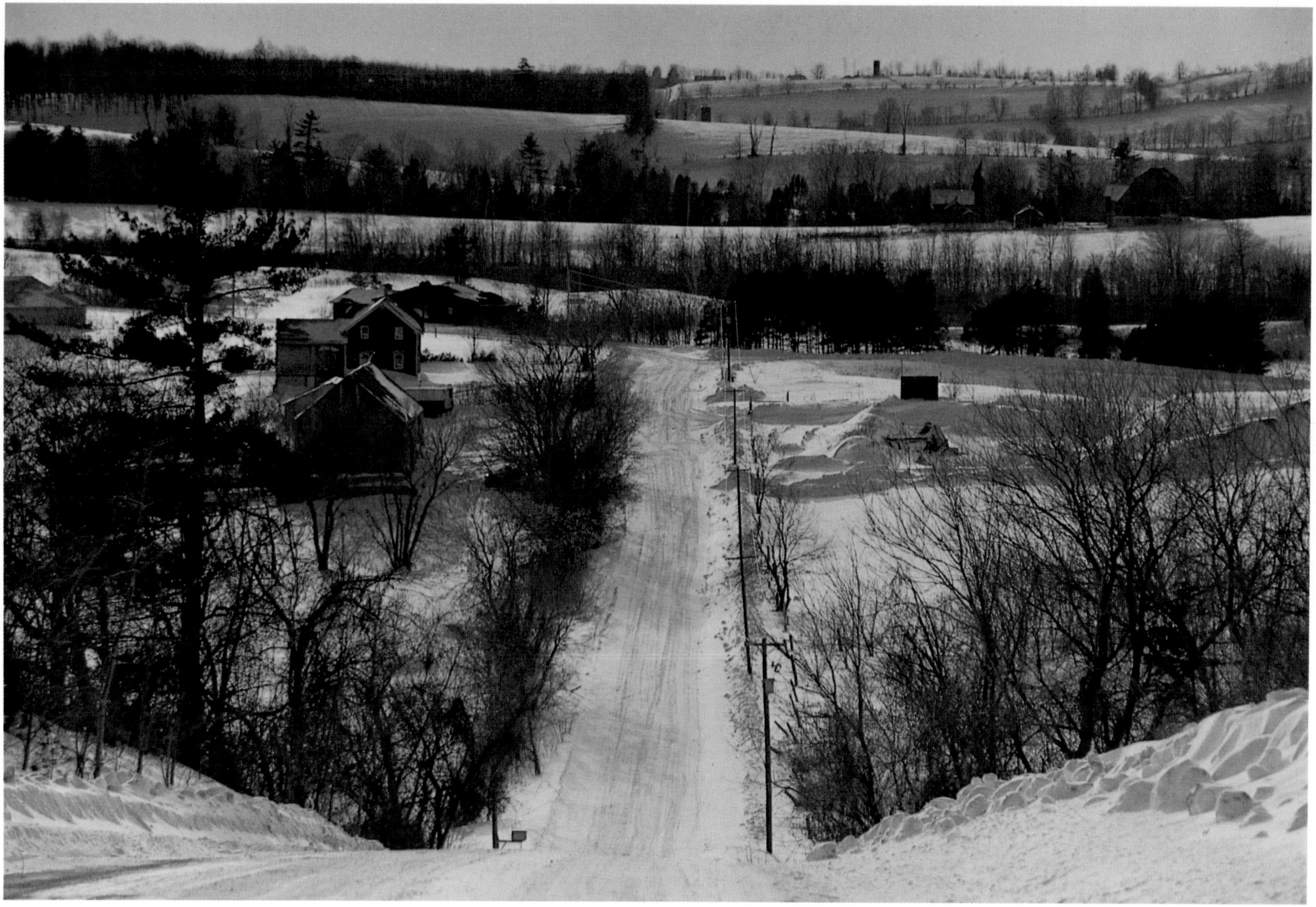

68 Near Warkworth

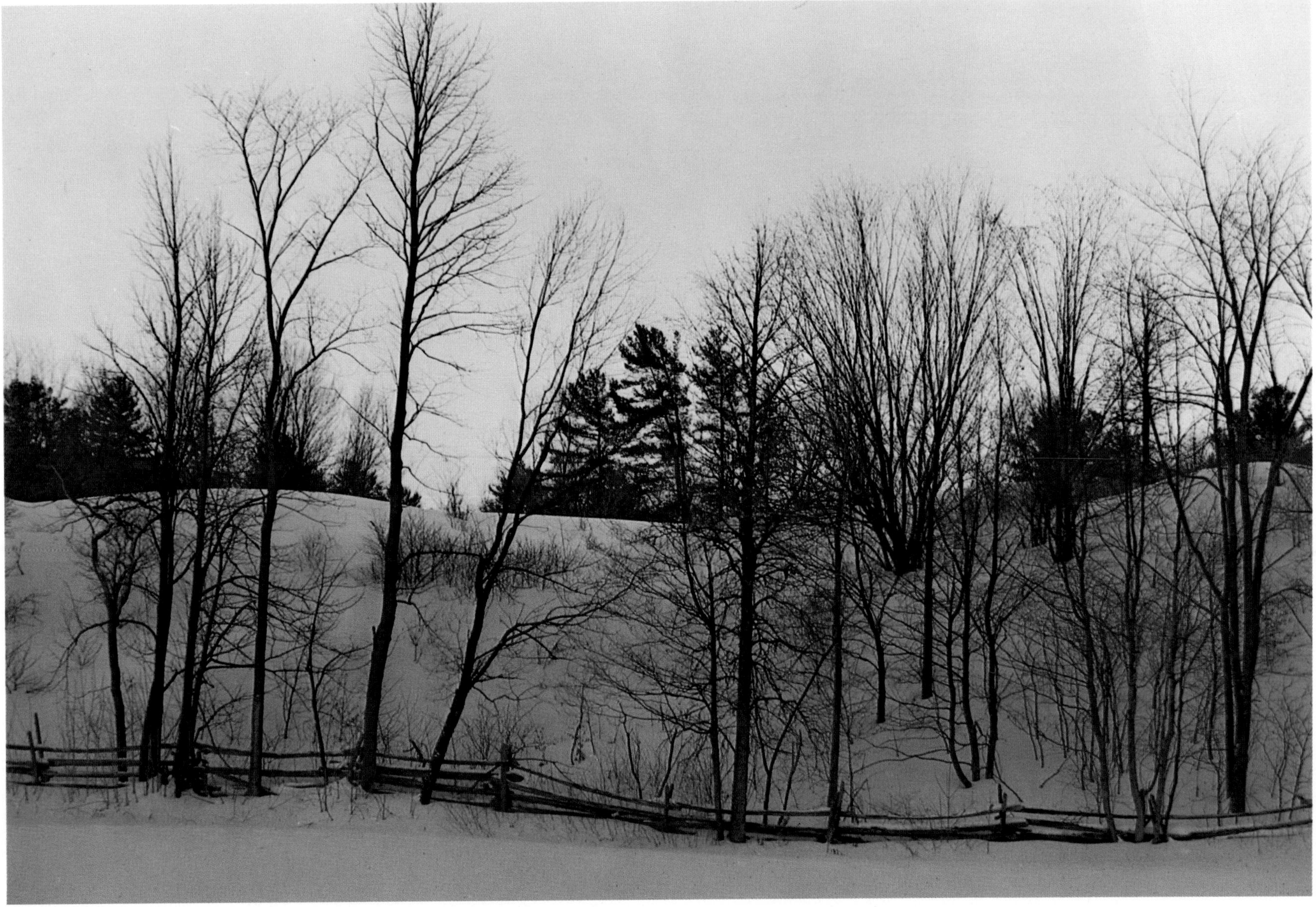

69 Near Hastings

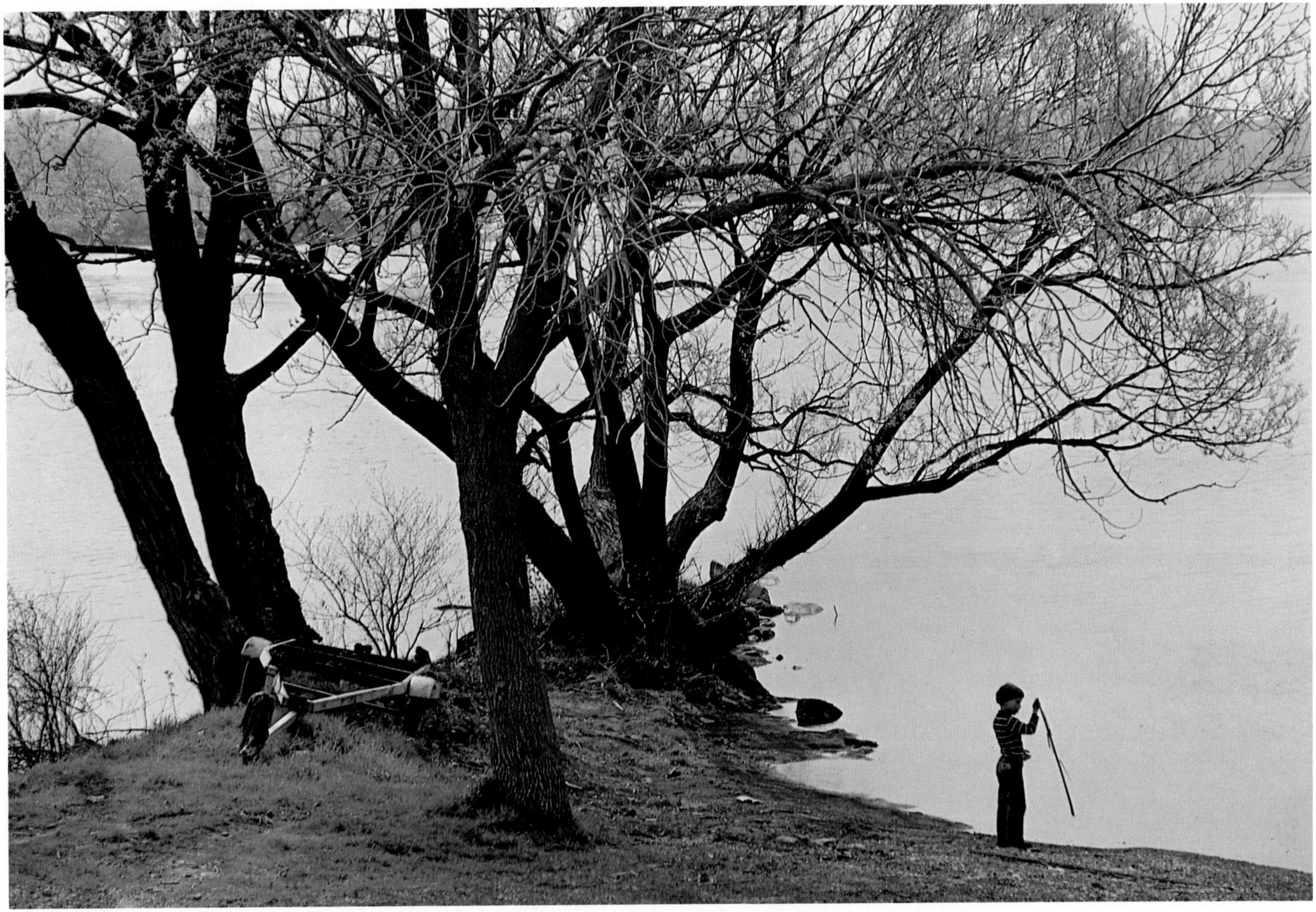

70 Near Rockport
71 Adolphustown

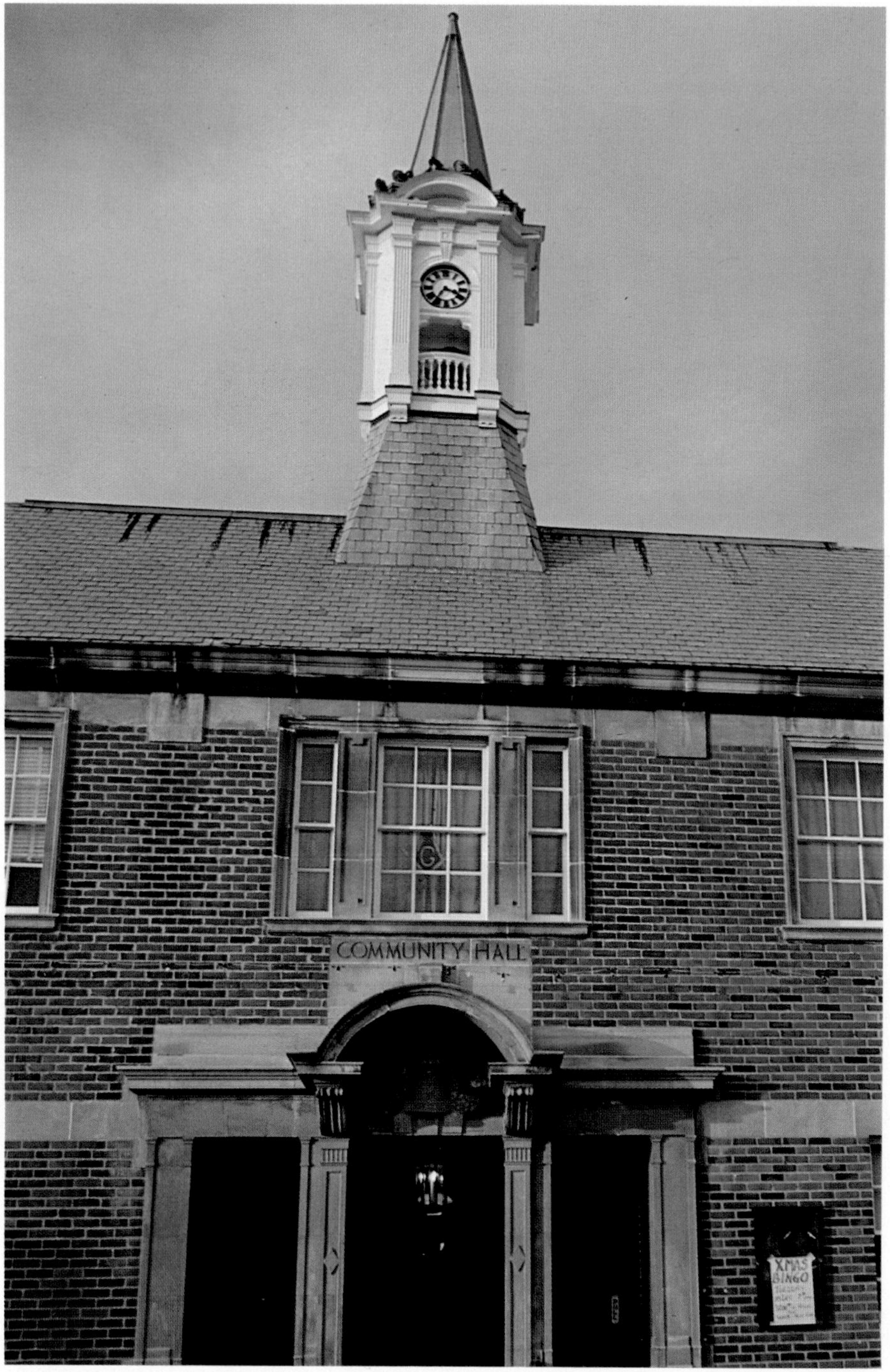
COMMUNITY HALL
XMAS
BINGO

72 Newcastle
73 Alan McPherson House, Napanee

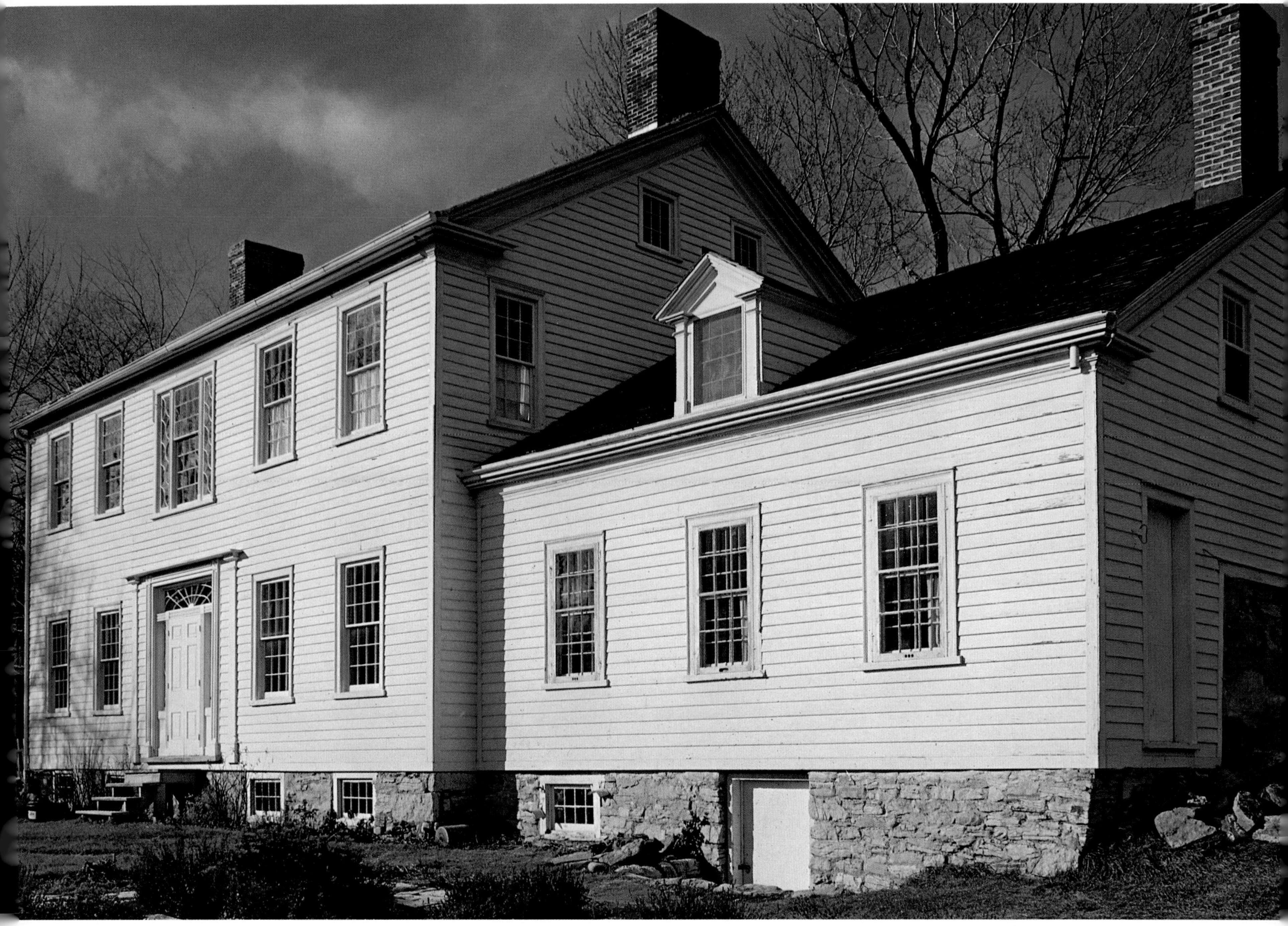

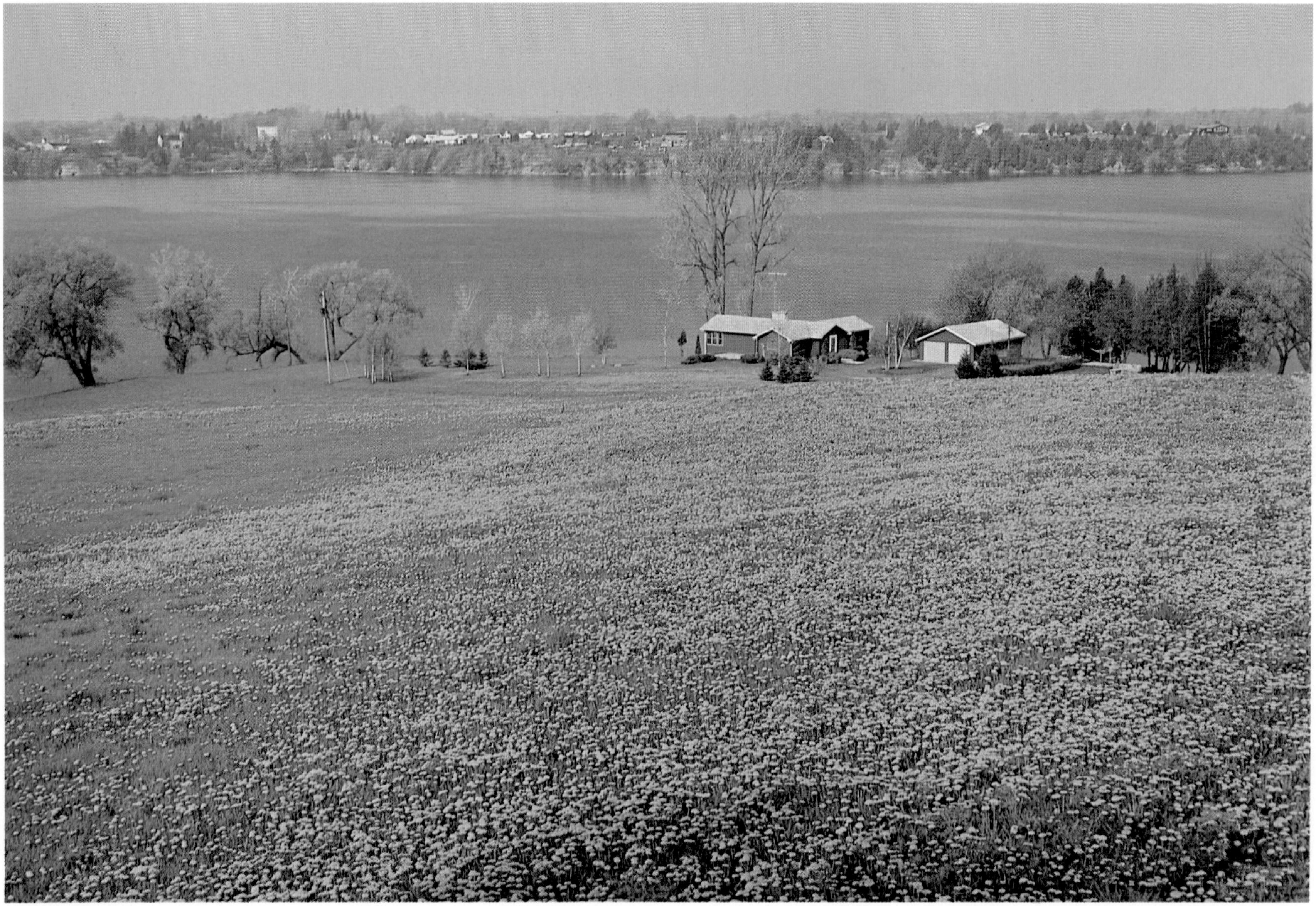

74 Near Glenora
75 Near Wicklow

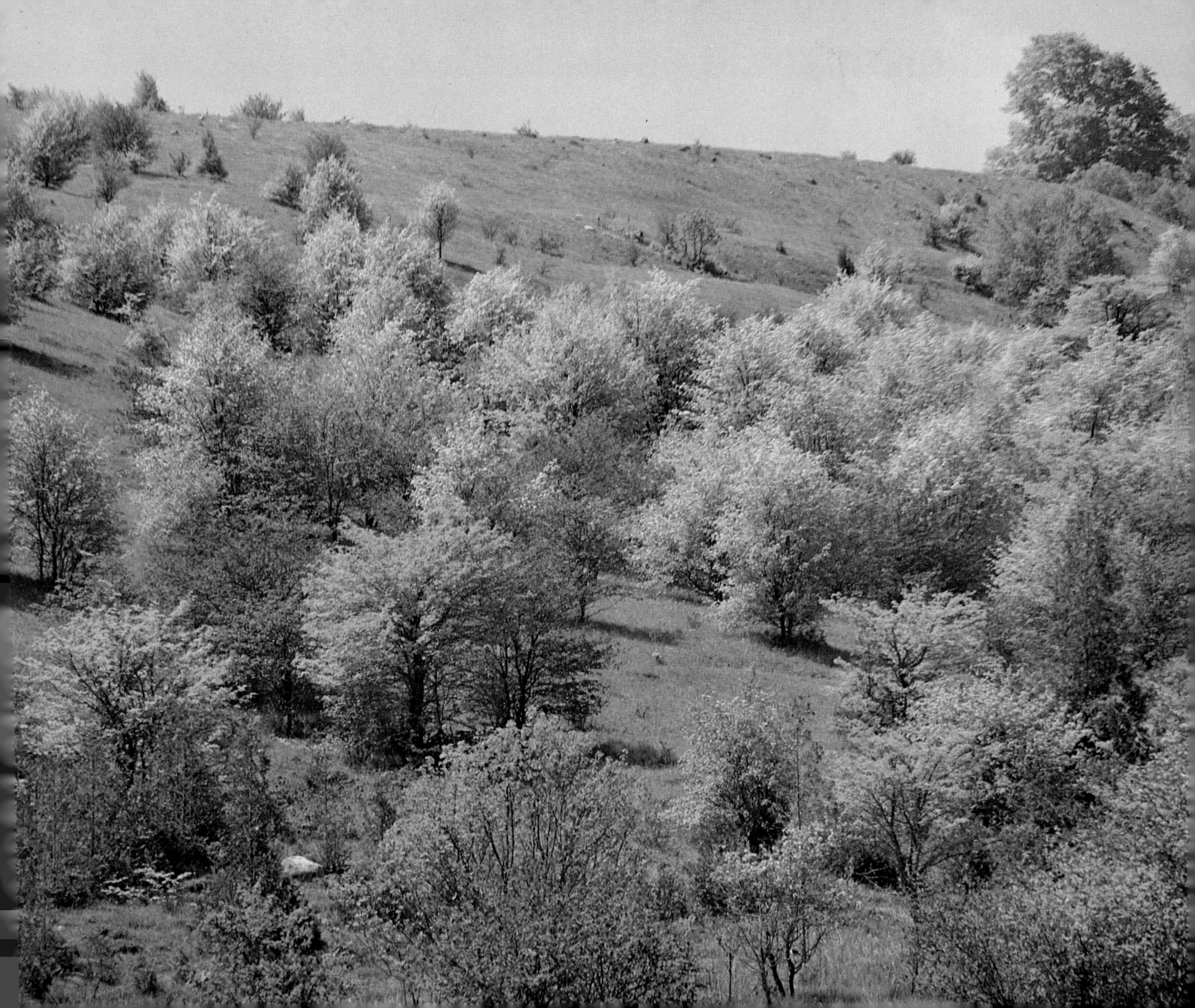

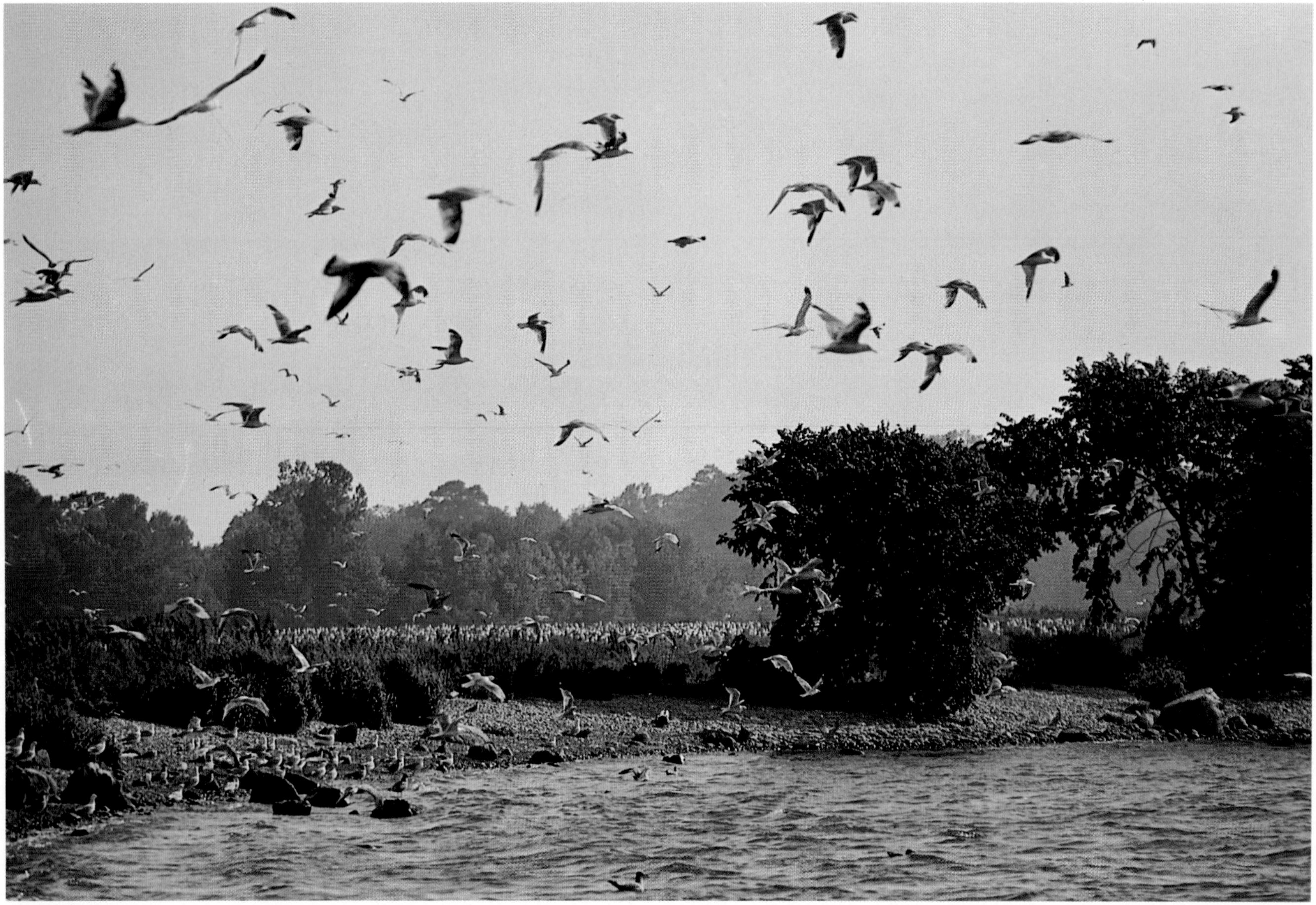

76 Presqu'Ile Provincial Park
77 Near Plainville

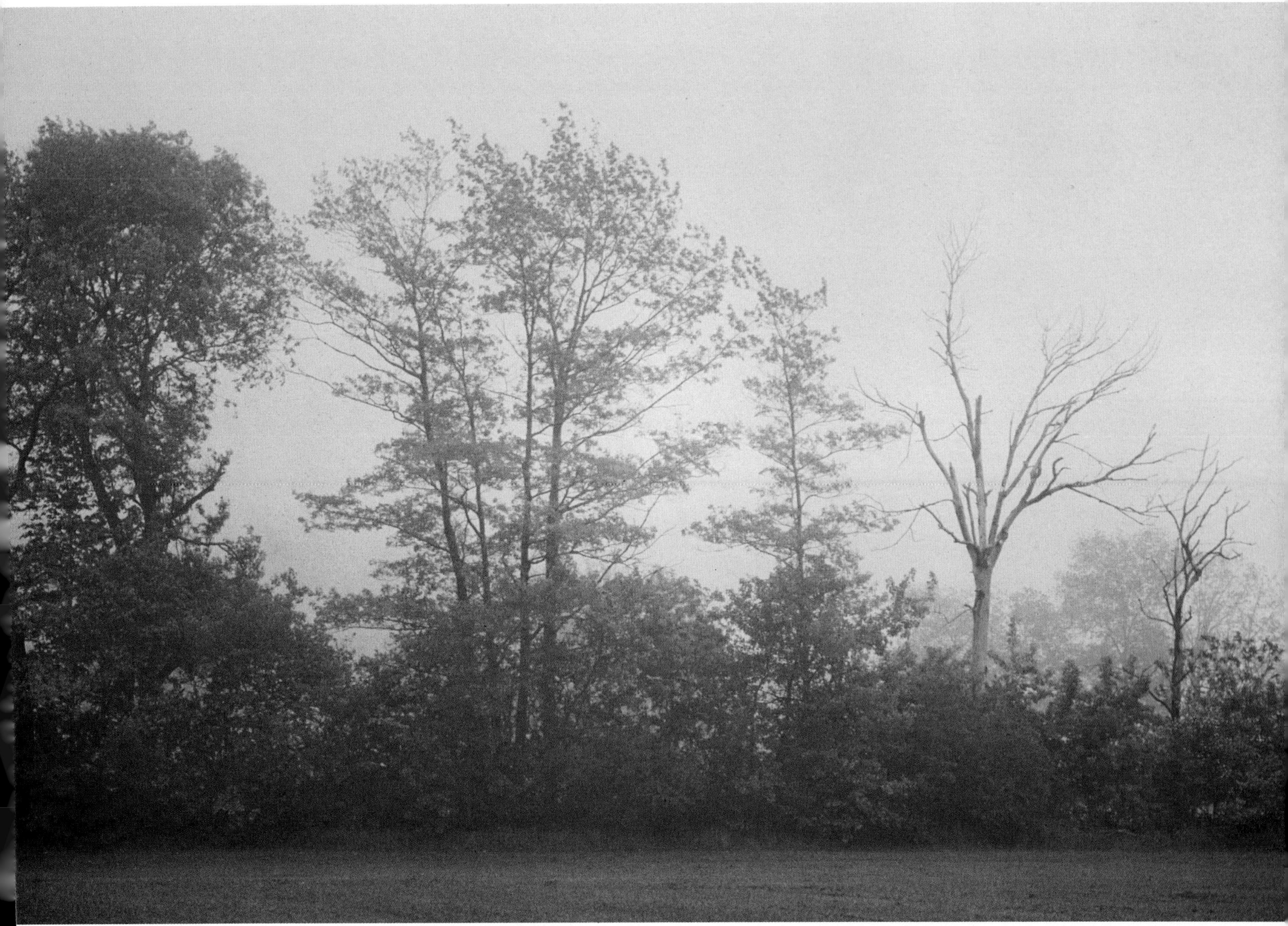

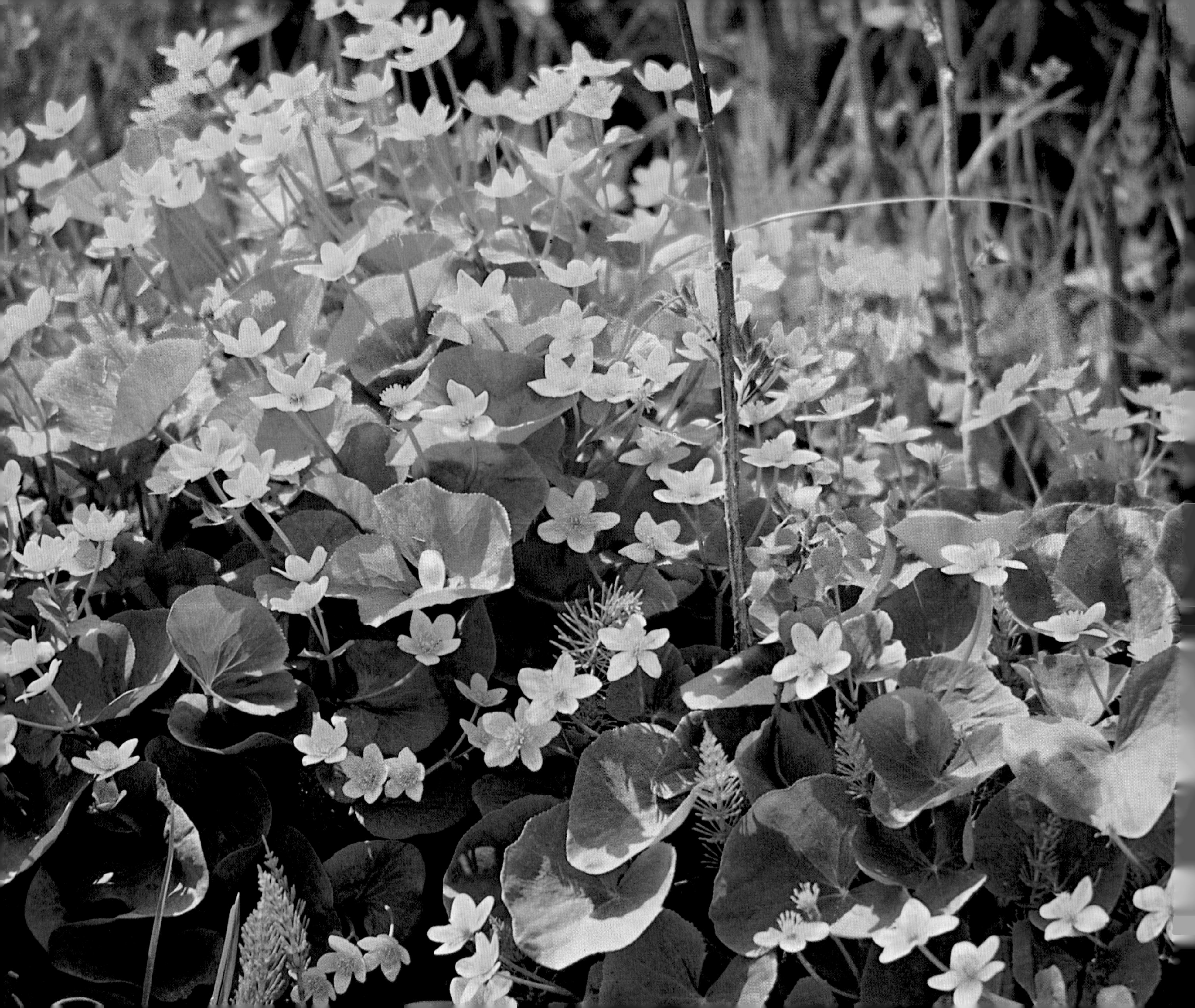

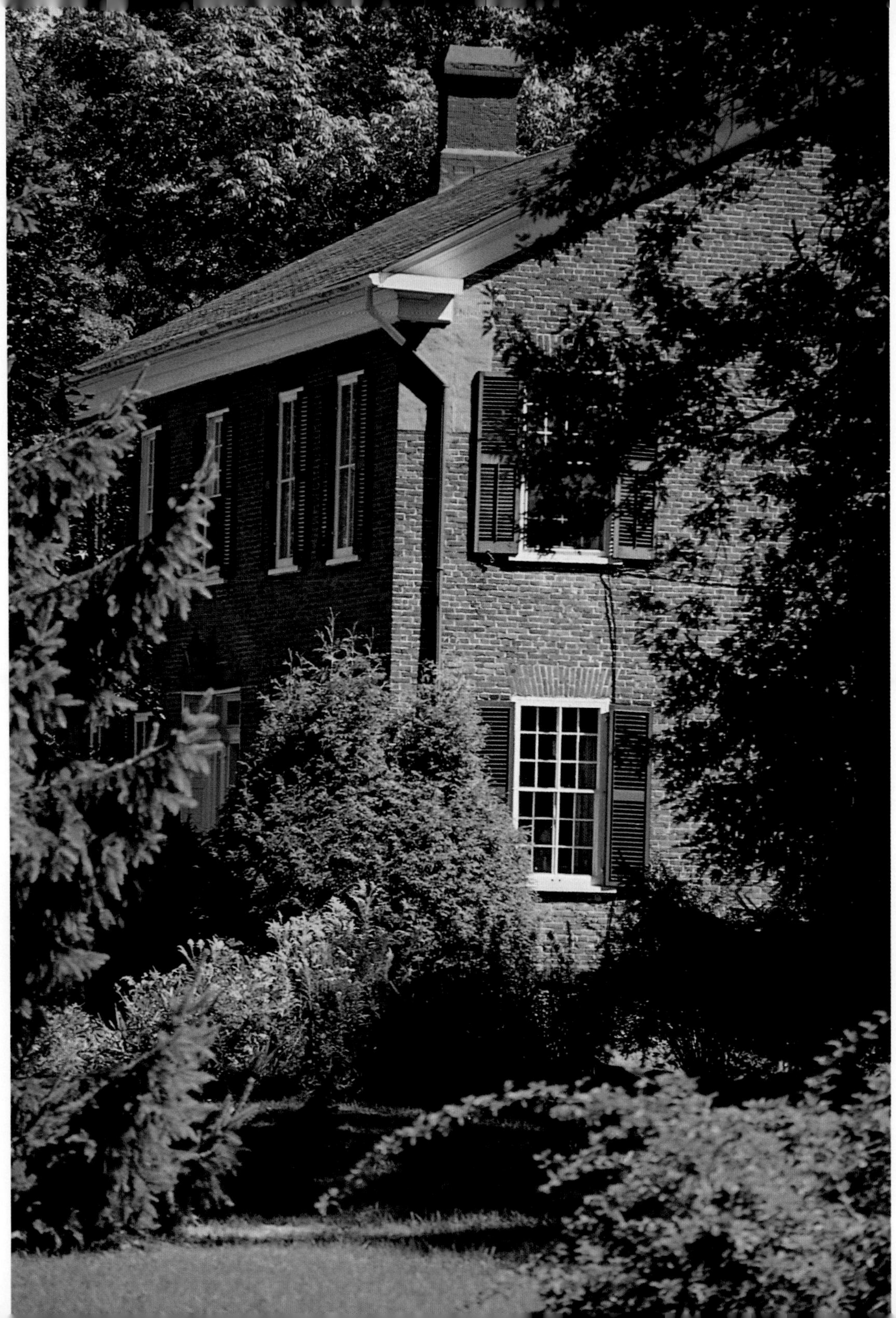

78 Dartford
79 Brimley House, Grafton

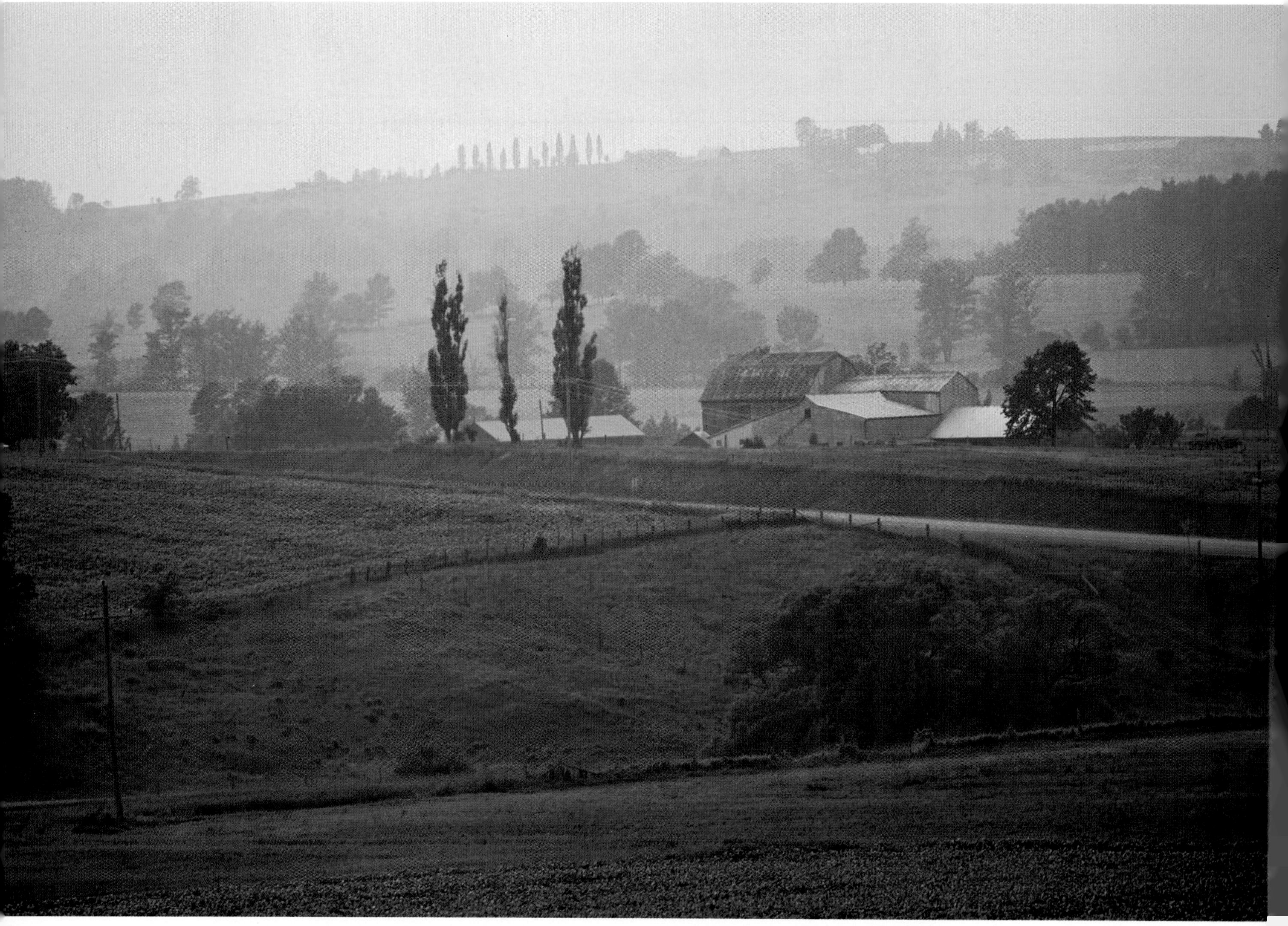

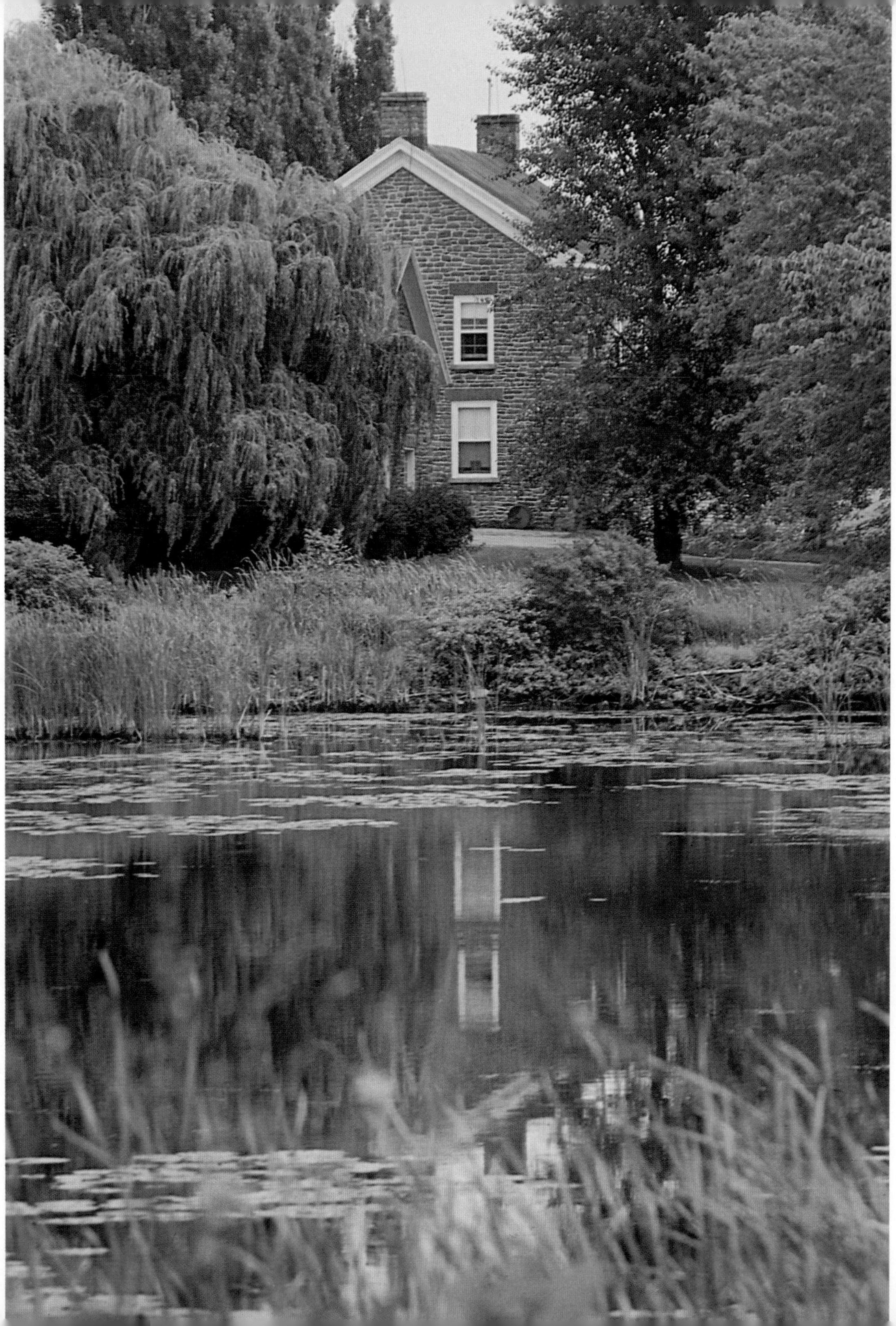

80 Near Baltimore
81 Near Iroquois

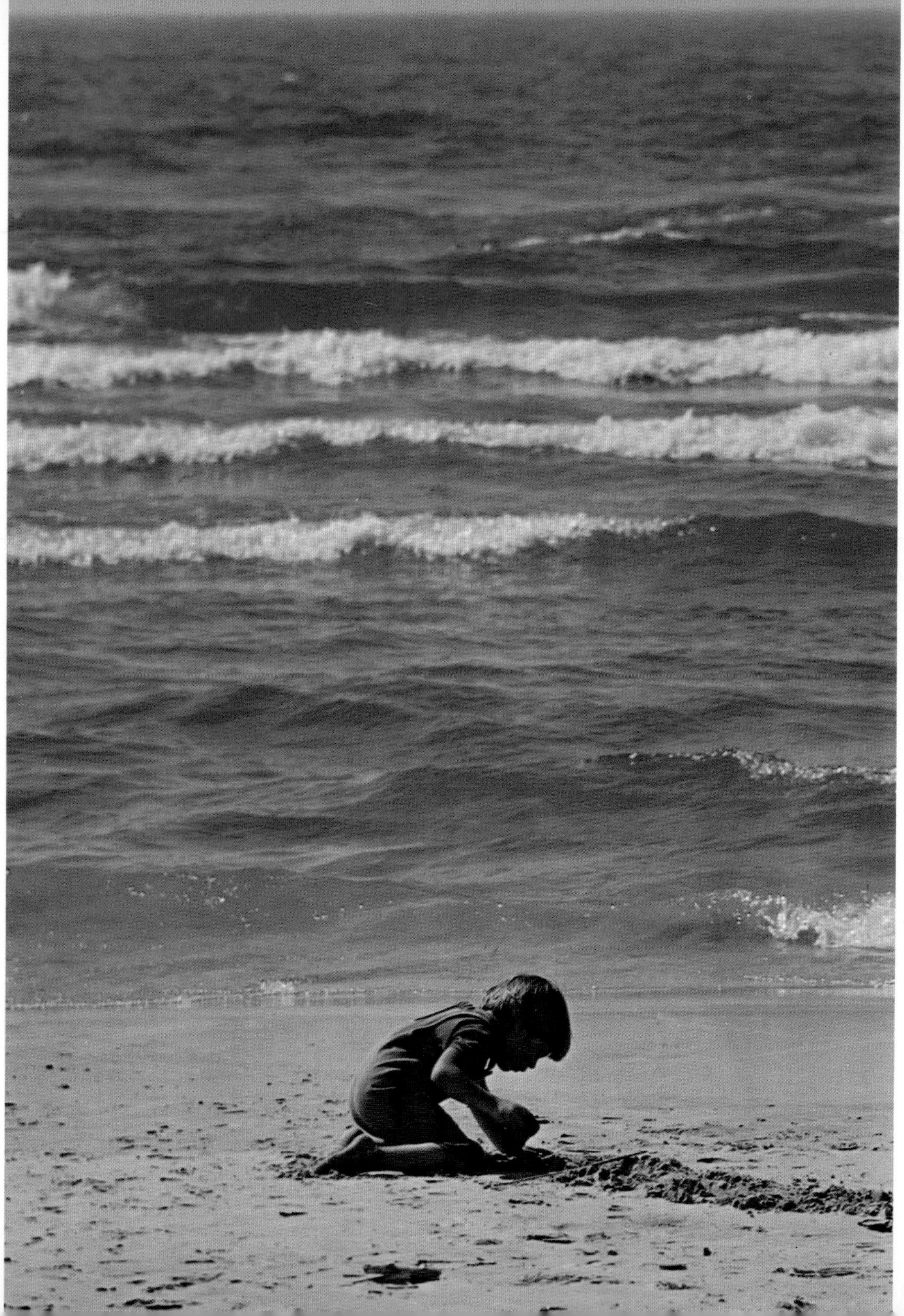

82 & 83 Sandbanks Provincial Park

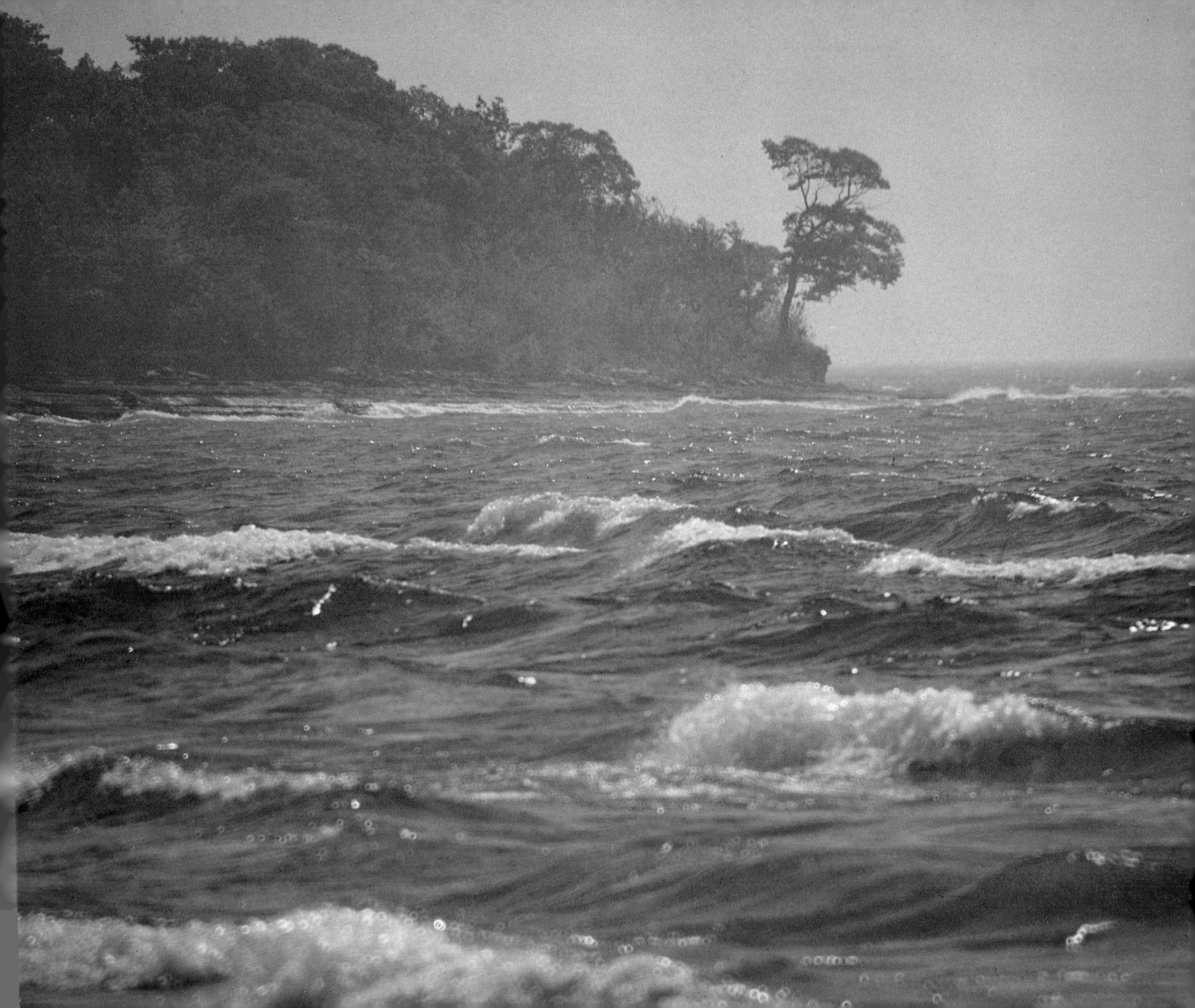

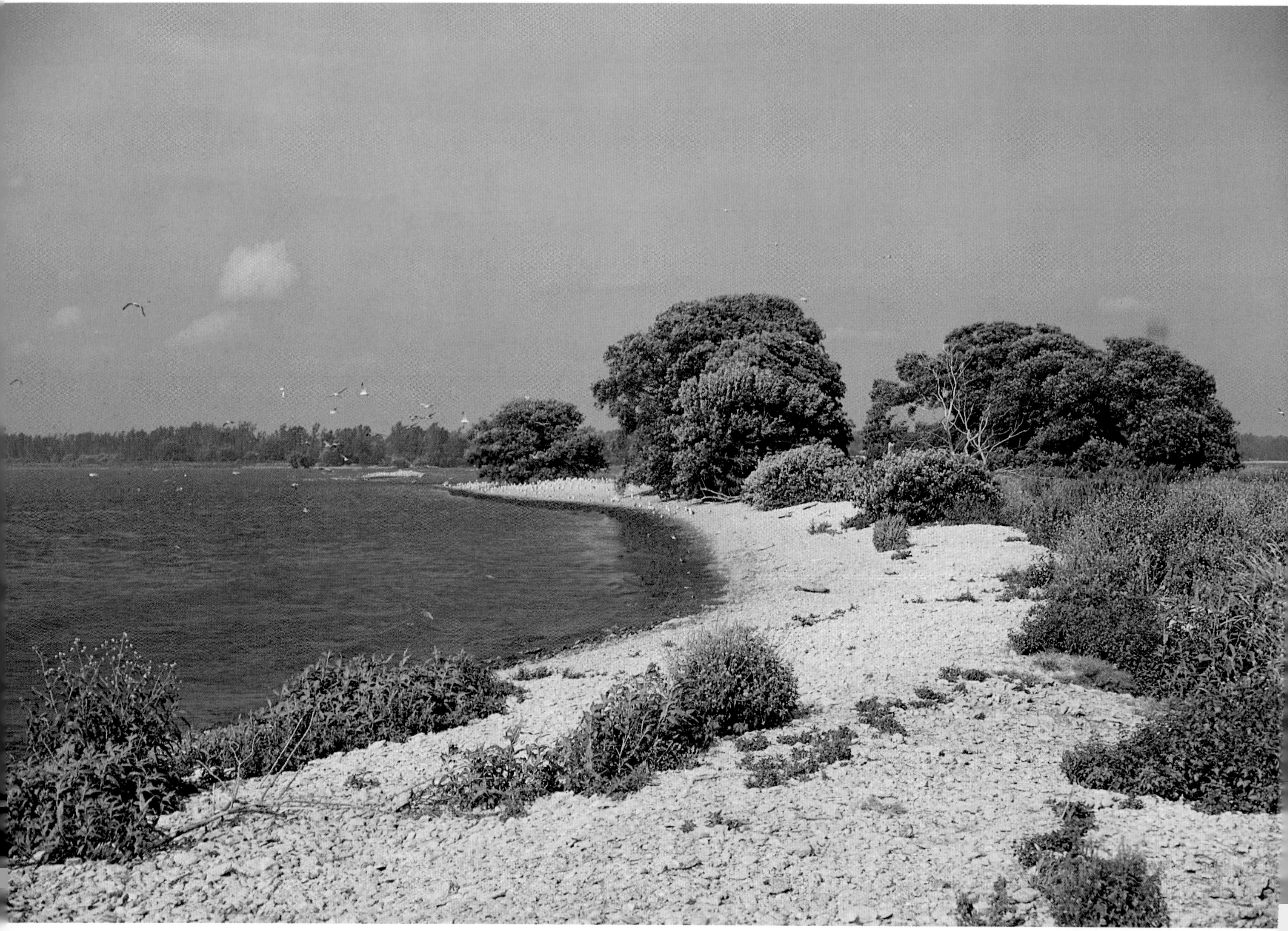

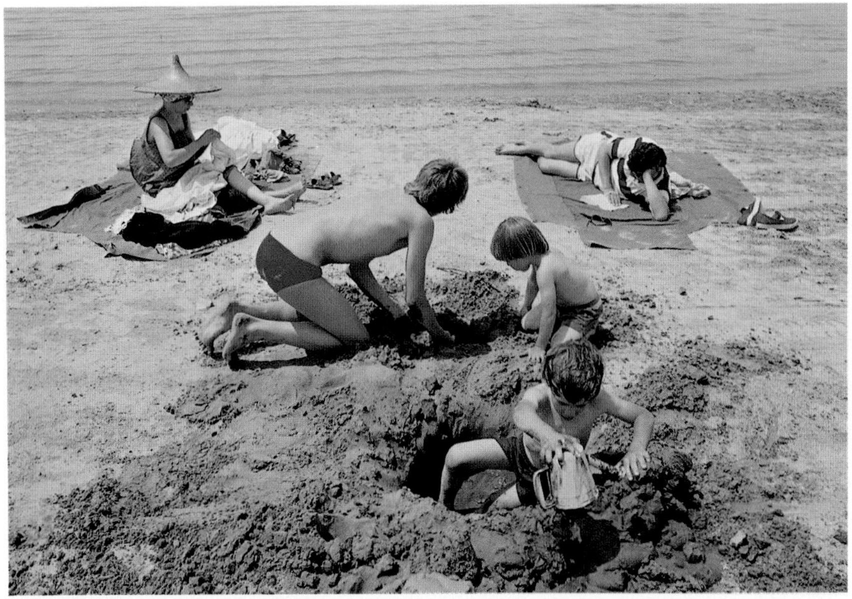

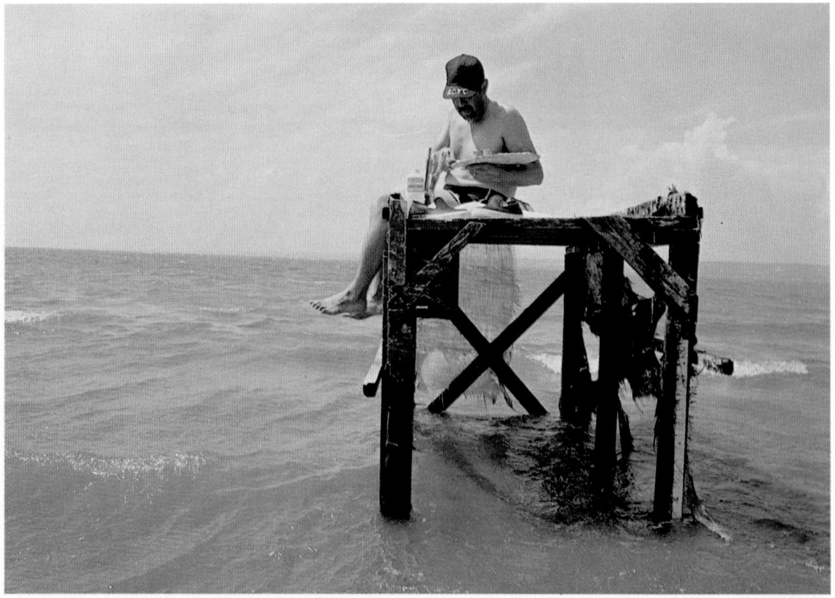

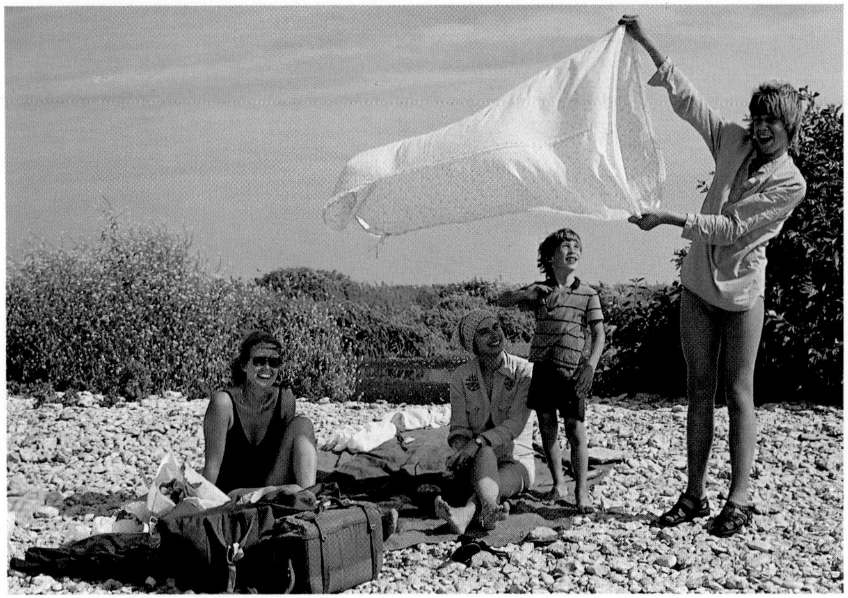

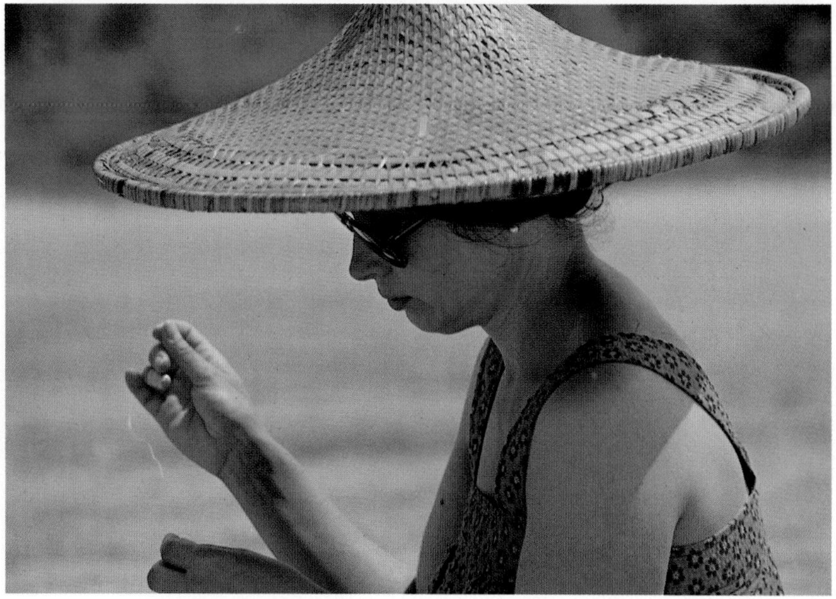

(over)
86 Presqu'Ile Provincial Park
87 Gore's Landing

84 & 85 Presqu'Ile Provincial Park

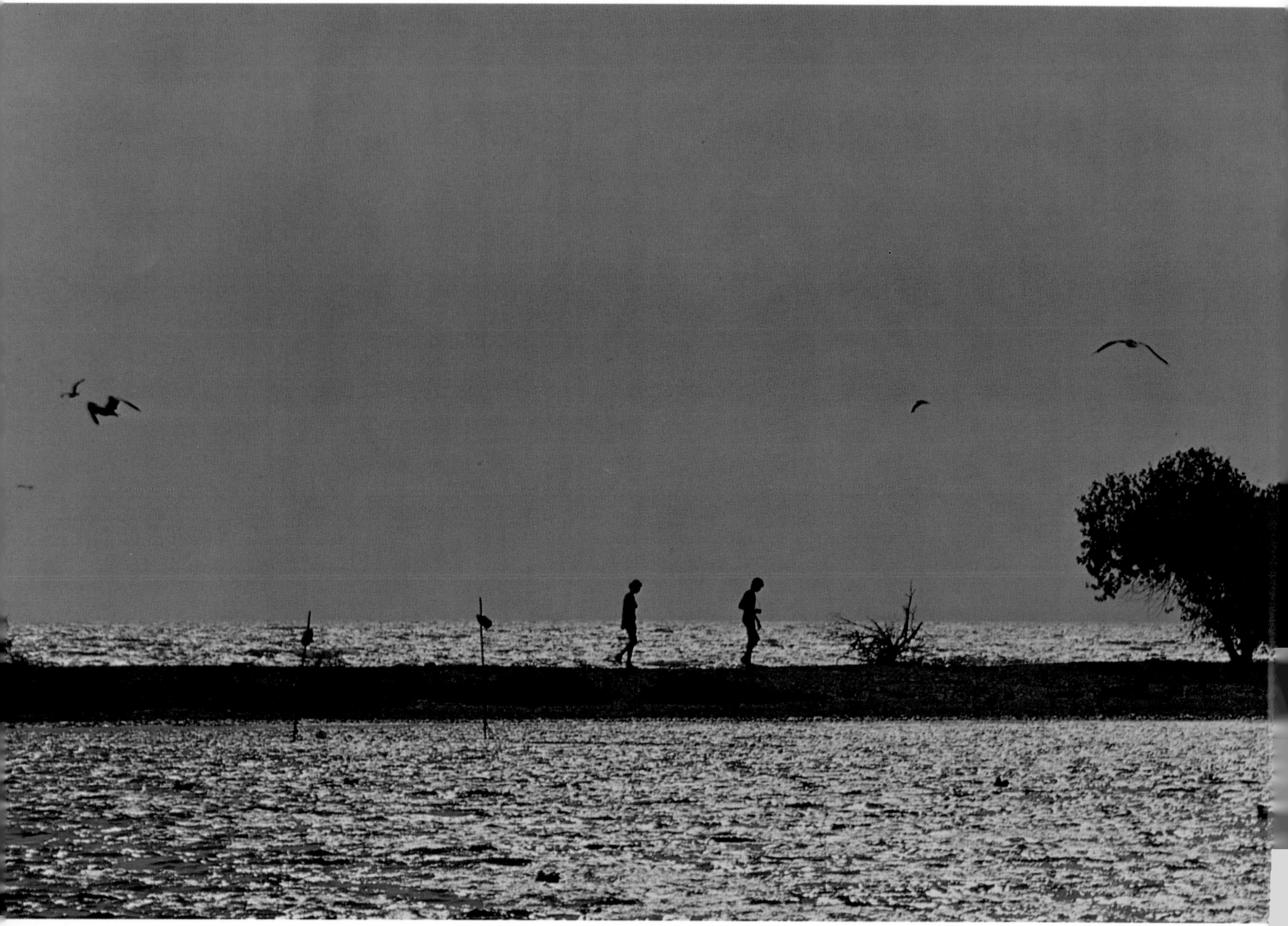

88   Rice Lake